GRIEVE
OUTSIDE THE BOX

GRIEVE
OUTSIDE THE BOX

A TRAVELING LADY SHAMAN'S A-Z GUIDE TO
EMBRACING THE DEATH DOULA WITHIN

ELENA BOX

Calliope
Commons

Cover Design: Samira Iravani
Art Direction: Morgane Leoni

First edition

For my father Richard Bruce Box.

Born: November 10th, 1952

Airborne: January 8th, 2016.

TABLE OF CONTENTS

INTRODUCTION:

How I Know What I Know

"MACHU PICCHU!" I cried out, dancing jubilantly in my kitchen. It was January 2016, and my father had just left his body from his hospice bed in the living room of my childhood home. Sitting next to his newly lifeless body, the room moved around me in a surreal scene.

My Mom and older sister Mia sat on the couch with an acoustic guitar. Everything seemed to be held up by an invisible force: a sort of pristine snow globe outside of time and space imbued with a special reverence and ease. Golden early morning light filtered through the white slatted shades. Dad was laying on his side, eyes closed, next to the drafting desk that belonged to the architect father before him. Everything felt incredibly ... alive.

At the foot of the bed, a golden framed painting of his mother was hanging, with her as a young girl in a short white dress sitting on a stone garden bench holding a single green apple. It was as if she was watching over him, in the moment a real-life Dali, a once-mundane portkey to some other plane of existence. Dad was wrapped in my favorite checkered baby blue blanket I'd used as a kid, his body now growing a pale bluish-grey. Mouth open. Ensconced in a liminal space, like the molecules of air were dancing a ballet to Carnival of the Animals by Saint Saëns.

One could travel to every luxury spa in the world and never quite find this kind of serenity. It was as if the whole world had paused between an inhale. Suspended. Another smell I cannot place permeated the room, and when I smell it on myself months later after a sweaty yoga class in Bali it makes me cry. Is it mucus? A portal smell? A newborn baby? What? If I could bottle it and smell it I would. Like ambergris. That somehow strangely delicious stank. Creamy and weird like a lover's crotch or sports bra. Nature's own oopsie daisy eau de parfum. Death and rebirth all in one.

Six months prior: I'm hiking in the Peruvian Andes. Walking along an ancient Incan path laid out thousands of years before me. Strapped into army green military hiking boots, a sapphire blue knock-off north face purchased in a Cusco Market, a puffy white alpaca fur hat, and a large hydrant red scarf. The Spanish women who trekked with my group pointed out that the "scarf" I'd purchased from a small boutique along the hilly cobble-stoned streets of Cusco looked more to them like a "manta" or blanket. They laughed and poked fun at me. Sure, I knew it was large but I wanted to create a cape-like effect as I climbed the rock-laden peaks, and traversed the rickety "incan bridges" over large crevasses held together only by what seemed to be sticks, rocks, and mud.

Upon returning home to Brooklyn, I laid the red alpaca wool blanket over my full-size bed, and indeed it was large enough to cover it comfortably. You all know fashion is key when embarking on adventures of epic proportions. But back to the trek: blanket or not, I was prepared to face my mountain. The journey was called "Ausangate" after the majestic mountain we would be climbing. The local native language of Quechua speaks to the mythology of this great mountain. It is also known as an "Apu," or sacred mountain. People spend their entire lives dedicated to learning from this guru-like behemoth. Capped with snow and sort of carved out along it's face, it looks like a great spot to take the sleigh ride of your life.

I'd left Brooklyn feeling stuck after successfully producing my first sketch-comedy pilot. I'm a character comedy actress, you see. Many nights of my early 20's were spent hunting down open mics on Macdougal street in New York's Greenwich Village. It was exhilarating. A strange world dominated by men where a short skirt and a smile could get you five minutes on stage in front of a crowd. I used the zeal I acquired in smooth-talking politicians during my time spent as a legislative assistant on Capitol Hill to woo my way into many a scene. A networker's dream. I'd bring characters I'd built as a child playing dress-up in the mirror. Friends I'd created to bestow the wisdom I lacked when going through the trauma of losing my family and witnessing 9/11.

I brought these zany weirdos to life for a moment of sweet salve by way of laughter to the audiences I met. Believing that if I could bring one moment of respite, my work would be worth it. After years on stage I birthed my characters into a pilot I planned to pitch in Hollywood. Only as I got it all wrapped up tightly in a bow, my entire world disintegrated. I was unsure about how to move forward with pitching my show when I knew that in a few months, my father would be dead.

His tumor had grown back after all the treatments, surgeries, and clinical trials. The man had become a human lab-rat for the sake of science. It felt wrong to go full steam ahead in the direction of my comedic dreams when my world felt so incredibly un-funny. How could I weave a world of adult diapers, chemotherapy, and brain surgeries into my comedy? I struggled to find the creative zest I needed to soldier on. I needed a spiritual kick in the ass so I could pull myself up by the bootstraps to pitch and sell this show.

Sensing that I had a little time before diving deeply into a world of hospice, I took a chance and flew to Peru to study plant medicine in the Amazon and then most importantly: climb a mountain. Enter: Apu Ausangate. I needed to conquer a literal mountain that represented the creative climb I wanted to take to overcome my stagnancy. I knew I needed to face a spiritual mountain to gain the tools necessary to face the moment of death.

We had gotten the call. We'd soon have to call it quits.

Airborne

I imagined him booming "airborne!" as Dad often did, a reference to his older, wilder days. "I used to jump outta airplanes, you know!" he'd remind any willing listener every chance he could get. In his thick southern drawl. It's a wonder that just a few months earlier, he was taking his last kamikaze-type flight out of an airplane. Against all odds and the doctor's wishes. My father, a six-foot-two Texan man with the most aggressive type of brain tumor, decided he needed to feel the wind beneath his wings just one last time on this earth.

It was year three of his journey through brain cancer. The doctors initially gave him three months and he gave that glioblastoma astrocytoma three wild years. After so much anticipation, the moment of death had become mythical to me. All the waiting made me think it was impossible to leave one's body. How to extract a soul out of seemingly solid matter? Surely this is some witchery! A quantum phenomenon. And yet, all living creatures since the beginning of time had seemed to have figured it out.

A few days before he died, I was sitting in my dining room glued to YouTube. I was replaying all the triumphant moments from the 90's movie *Free Willy*. This was my attempt at a rehearsal of death as my father laid in the room beside me, in a coma, his loud death rattle my soundtrack. After being in captivity for years, 6-ton Orca whale Willy claims his freedom in one glorious moment as he victoriously leaps over a rock wall and into the sea. Beneath him, Jesse, his unlikely 12-year-old friend, cheers him on. Jesse pumps his fist in the air screaming "YEAH!" in slow motion.

I was trying to understand what was about to happen. How it *could* happen. The fabled event of death.

Your Own Pace is Grace

The first night of the Peruvian expedition, my international trekking group reached the base camp of Apu Ausangate, a mountain so holy that it has a consciousness of its own. My body was weak after my months-long dieta and Ayahuasca ceremonies, but I did my best hiking my way up into the mountains. Coming from the humid and tropical Amazon, the shift into the snow covered rocky grounds that met us at the feet of Ausangate was a bit of a shock.

We'd hiked an incline for about 5 hours to reach this spot and I found a large boulder alongside a babbling stream that flowed beside the valley beneath the mountain. I laid on my back and stared at the face of the mountain while listening to the flowing water. I felt something gurgling within my belly and felt pain beginning to spread within my guts. All day I had been drinking water from my Nalgene bottle that I'd taken from the hot water dispenser at my hostel before we left. I'd been filling my bottles at night with hot water and sleeping with them to stay warm then drinking them during the day.

Already I'd had a few days of an upset stomach but I hadn't put two and two together. I figured the water had been boiled so surely it was good enough to drink? Hostel guests used it to make their Coca Leaf tea to help with altitude sickness. Surely I would be fine, I thought to myself as I laid on the rock. In the distance, trekking horses watched our guides play a rowdy game of fútbol as the sun set. Little did I know, these little rumblings would be the precursor to a night of trials at the foot of this wise mountain.

As we prepared for bed, our guides cautioned us to wait a moment before using the outhouse at night. They said the freezing temperatures combined with the altitude could cause you to pass out if you don't sit up and let your body adjust first. "No problem!" I thought.

When we got to our tents I noticed something was missing. A crucial something. In an effort to pack light, I'd forgone my sleeping bag and decided to rent one with the trekking company before leaving Cusco. Only problem was, my guides did not get the memo.

Distressed, I confronted them, two kind young men with the legs of swift mountain lions. One, who went by the name of "Puma" tried to calm me. He pulled out an extra bag he'd brought. Holding it up I could see it was made for a small child. It would barely cover my legs. The chef called me into his cooking hut and poured boiling hot water into my Nalgene water bottles. Like little coals to cuddle through what would prove to be a harrowing night. We smoked cigarettes together as he assured me all would be well, though his face told another story. He was worried.

My tent was shared with a kind older Mexican woman. She barely spoke English and my Spanish was a little rusty. We got ready for bed. She was tucked into her large sleeping bag, snug as a bug. And there I was, dressed in every piece of clothing I'd brought covered barely by the sleeping bag and hugging my bottles fiercely. Already they were losing heat. The pain coursed through my abdomen and I struggled to hide it. My tent-mate offered me what medicines she'd come prepared with. Something for altitude sickness. I wasn't sure. I took it and laid down.

Closing my eyes two things became very clear to me: I was *really* freaking cold, and I was incredibly with-out-a-doubt severely ill. What began as a spiritual trek quickly turned into a tribulation. Throughout the evening I made frantic dashes into the snow to visit the outhouse. A small hole dug into the frozen ground. Everything within me was roiling. I was being turned completely inside out. Up and out, I unzipped our tent and ran beneath the stars to visit this hole. Overhead was the milky way and the most wonderful array of stars one could imagine. Watching me carefully was the white-faced mountain, electrically lit by the full moon above. Was it mocking my misfortune?

My poor tent mate barely got a wink of sleep either as the moment I laid down to shiver beneath my "sleeping bag", my guts told me it was time to get up and get out again. I'd forgotten all about the caution to slowly rise because mama did *not* have time for that. At one point, our dear tent had enough of my comings and goings and the zipper broke completely, leaving the two of us totally bare and exposed to the snow and wind outside.

Surrendering to the lesson, I returned to my lukewarm water bottles and curled up. I had a moment of clarity amidst the hellish night. I thought to myself: "If I can get through this, I can get through anything."

As dawn broke and the rest of the camp began to stir, I thanked all my guides, ancestors, and of course our dear Apu who watched over me and gave me one of the toughest lessons of my life. I was exhausted and completely tapped out. But spirit had one more assignment for me that would restore my confidence and spirit. Looking around the bloodshot and weary eyes of my fellow travelers as we gathered for our morning Coca leaf tea, I could see a number of them had also not fared very well either. They were experiencing severe altitude sickness. Up here the air was thin. Like you could sip in the largest breath of your life and still find yourself gasping for more. It made people sick to their stomachs.

Our guides rounded up a few horses from the valley and called our group to gather. "Who knows how to ride a horse?" he asked. It was clear these people had no strength in them to climb the next leg of the tour and would have to be taken up by horseback. Looking around I could see that not a single one of them raised their hands. My hand shot up: "Yo puedo!" My years of summer camp training would come in handy. And so off we went up the side of the great Apu on our horses. I led the group in my large black-rimmed sunglasses, puffy alpaca hat, and waving red blanket cape. Behind me trailed a sorry-looking crew of travelers so ill they were literally vomiting off the side of their horses down the 200 foot drops below them.

I was exhausted without a wink of sleep the night before though I had a task: I had to get these people safely up to the top of the mountain. Armed with the might and strength I'd been gifted through my gut-wrenching ordeal, I knew: "Puedo hacer esto." Once we got to Aguas Calientes, we spent the night in the first real bed I'd seen in days. We awoke at three in the morning to begin our climb up to the ancient site: Machu Picchu.

My legs were completely burnt out and I was running on fumes at this point. The Australian doctor who accompanied me was a kind, ginger-haired young lady and stuck with me while she could. Eventually, seeing that I was trailing behind, she politely asked if she could go ahead. One by one, in the cool darkness of the early morning, other pilgrims passed me in their headlamps. I was moving like a snail. My ego told me: "Come on, keep up! What is wrong with you?" I tried with all my might to take the next step a bit faster. But I could not move any quicker than my body could carry me. I reached a moment when I profoundly understood that it was okay to take my time. I was in competition with no one. And hypothetically, the monument had been around for thousands of years, so surely it would still exist by the time I got there, no? The morning sun began to rise as I climbed, step by step. Up and up into the tree line until I could take in an expansive view of the lush green Andes just catching the early golden light.

Wild dogs accompanied my trek. With no other humans in sight, they cheered me on with every grueling step I took. Some would trot along with me for a few minutes, then trade me off to be overseen by the next little mongrel. Others stayed longer, assuring me as I carried on, muscles weak and heart strength fading. Finally, halfway up the mountain, I had a thought: "Machu Picchu doesn't exist! How could it?"

After all, I had been hiking for literal days and I had not reached it yet. All this time I had been lied to. All the documentaries and photographs I had seen were complete *garbage* and I was being tricked all along! I was *convinced*. I paused and looked at the small brown dog by my side. We laughed. He knew it too. Machu Picchu was a mirage! "Still," I thought, "I'm here now, the only way up is up so I might as well keep going." Completely certain that Machu Picchu no longer existed and perhaps never existed,

I journeyed on, dogs by my side ... until finally, with the sun fully rising in the sky, I somehow summited the mountain.

In front of me was an expanse of blinding white rocks piled into a large sparkling city stretching out in front of me. It looked simultaneously small and entirely vast. It looked exactly like all the postcards and documentaries had shown, only it was real. It was here. Amongst the ruins were humans. Tourists! My group of fellow trekkers stood atop the ancient civilization proudly posing for photos with smiling faces. A few told me they'd skipped the climb and opted for the shortcut: a bus. What a laugh! All that time a bus could have chauffeured me up to the top of that mythical mountain. Still, though, I valued the journey. I valued the doubt. I valued the sweat, the tears, *and* the fears.

The journey was the lesson.

Who needs shortcuts anyway?

A Rolling Stone

I returned to this knowledge as we entered the liminal space that is a human's final moments on this earth plane.

I sat sipping coffee in the early morning on one unseasonably warm day in January 2016, beside my father's hospice bed ... reflecting on my climb. I'd spent every night for the last seven days next to his bedside witnessing the most miraculous visions and moments. His bed was licked by golden flames lit up by a nearby candle yet maximized by the presence of Spirit in the space. Visitors from the beyond came to carry him through. We straddled the space in between, together.

I had sensed which night would be his final one and asked my mother to spend it with him. Before going to bed I played him old videos of The Beatles performing in their suits and matching haircuts. I woke up with a start that morning on the couch looking out at the view of bare trees beyond the backyard. This morning was different. After three years of being in the space of illness, with the constant looming presence of death sitting with us every second of every day: the time had come.

My father had awoken from his preparatory coma that morning. He could no longer speak, still, his presence was clear. In his eyes was a peaceful sadness. Knowing it was time to say goodbye. We knew it to be true.

We gathered around him with coffee cups and a guitar to sing for him over the next hour or so. Country western tunes he had serenaded us with during his lifetime as a member of the "Corduroy Cowboy Company" band. Tears streamed down our faces as he squeezed our hands with the might of a hot-blooded and virile stag. Where did all this strength come from? The night before he had laid practically lifeless, naked on the bed, as we changed him one last time. He was a large man and it was quite a team effort. Now here was this same man, fully aware, fully awake for his final moments on earth.

We sang to him his closing song. "Lonesome Fugitive" by countryman Merle Haggard.

"I'd like to settle down, but they won't let me
A fugitive must be a rolling stone
Down every road there's always one more city
I'm on the run, the highway is my home
I'm on the run, the highway is my home"

At the final strokes of the guitar strings, he looked me deeply in the eyes. I gazed back.

I summoned the strength of Free Willy, and all the wisdom I'd won through climbing the mountains of this journey, and pierced my gaze through his. I pushed my vision through his eyes and blasted him with love and courage. "You can do this!" I told him through my heart and mind.

WHOOSH.

He was airborne. He had done it. Death existed. And he journeyed on.

He had existed — and then so beautifully, so delicately, like pouring warm milk into a teacup, he was no more. Left behind was a vessel. And that — was something to celebrate.

I leapt up, danced into the kitchen, and exclaimed: "MA-CHU PICCHU!"

It was real. I had lived it.

And this is how I know what I know.

The Middle Road, Toad

In college, I had a professor who was Mormon. Every day he came to class completely buttoned up from head to toe. Even in the warmer months, he wore long sleeves and pants. We never saw more than his neck and hands. He never drank, he never swore, and he had never touched a sip of coffee because of its mind-altering effects. Although he allowed himself one indulgence. Every Sunday, he confessed to me that one day in his office, he would eat a handful of cocoa-dusted almonds. He forgave himself of this one small sin each week. The minute amount of caffeine within the cocoa was permissible to him. All other deviations were not.

I idolized his measure. His ability to devote himself toward a single focus and dedication to his God. What he taught me was just that. Focus, follow the right path, and you will be absolved. You were perfect. If I just followed a set of rules, of how life was supposed to be mastered, I would be doing it right. With a solemn rigidity. This was the way. My world came crashing down when I returned to the University after a year abroad in London.

A fog of rumors swirled around about my esteemed professor. He had left his wife and three sons for a 21-year-old classmate of mine. This hurt. This man who I had put up on a pedestal as a model of strength, of moral righteousness, of fine character was demoted to nothing more than a horny teenager, living out his secret fantasies. He traded in his magical underwear for super-hero graphic tees. As you can guess, I'm still a bit salty about it to this day.

"How does this apply to a book about death?" I hear you ask.

When we hold ourselves too tightly to a set of rules, holy or otherwise, we are doomed to unravel. I've come to understand the soft approach to life is the way we must encounter death. A loose grip. The middle path.

"With empty hands I take hold of the plow."
Mahasattva Fu

While searching for a book to ease my suffering and help me understand what I was facing, I found myself stumped. All the books seemed to approach the subject of death with the same sense of drudgery. A slow march with one's head held low. Doom! Gloom! Disaster. No thanks!

The books I found were written for older people, in their twilight years, facing the big sleep. And here I was, barely 23, asking some big questions while my friends went out to bars and bedded one-time lovers. Where was the book for young folk? More and more friends come to me looking for answers. For ways to support our parents, our grandparents, our aunts and uncles. Young people, too, need a guide. A friend. And some laughs.

In my view, something so natural, and inherent within all the joys that life has to offer shouldn't be so grave (pun most definitely intended)! Surely we can allow ourselves a full bar of chocolate, a tall glass of wine, and a bit of fun!

"Life is hard," I hear you say.

After all, isn't this what we have been taught?

But what if it isn't? What if we can approach the death of a loved one with the same sense of levity we embodied as a newborn babe? Eyes wide open, giggling and babbling. Eager to be amazed by every new offering the universe had in store that day. We were alive, we will die. And when we allow it to be ... isn't this wild ride fun?

This book is an offering to the self I was in those days.

After my father's diagnosis with terminal brain cancer. After his death, I solo traveled through Australia and Bali. Searching. For what? A guide. A tool-kit. A life raft! How the heck do we do this thing called "Death"? In all my studies as a yogi, an actress, a political correspondent on Capitol hill, I had yet to find the answer to my question. Our society leaves vague answers and we have many questions to ask. Limiting answers to unravel.

Where has the ritual of death gone? Where is the acknowledgment of this rite of passage? I felt myself wondering why so many people held their heads at a tilt when they addressed me, so sad, when what I witnessed my father achieve in death was a heroic feat!

These questions urged me on to the next level of inner and outer study. I dove into ancient texts like The Tibetan Book Of The Dead, I studied with Balinese healers, I learned shamanic energy healing practices, heck, I even became a certified death doula to boot! My life became ensconced with death. In a good way! I sought answers and within this guide is a humble spattering of my discoveries. I claim to be no expert. I offer simply what I know.

This book is a guide to open an allowing within you to grieve in your own way. To give you permission to throw caution to the wind and say: "Fuck it! I'm grieving and this may not be how our culture intends it to look like, but here I am muthalickas!" Grief, in my belief, is not black and white. It is filled with just as many colors and iterations as we can behold within both the seen and unseen worlds. What I offer to you is another way. A sort of choose your own adventure. Because that's how this life is. Isn't it?

SO...HOW DO I USE THIS BOOK?

This handy book is a tool for you to navigate the depths of your grief. Within it, you'll find anecdotes, self-care rituals, meditations, and breathing techniques.

It is not meant to be read front to back, though you're welcome to, if you wish.

This book is meant to be enjoyed like a playlist on shuffle.

Choose the chapter that fits your current state.

What are you struggling with right now? What part of your grief are you feeling super alone with? My prayer is that within these pages you will find your special salve. A life raft in the part that is speaking to you the most.

Carry this book in your purse as you go about your day. When a wave of emotion feels imminent, open it up, and pour it out. The book is here to be a catcher for your tears. Let these pages soak them up when a shoulder to cry on is scarce. Who needs tissues anyway?

Also great for crying in public. If anyone asks, you can tell them the book is just a real tearjerker.

This book is also here for the friends of grieving people. Truth is, we will all go through this at some point and so if you are the friend of someone who is experiencing loss, think of this as a sort of training ground. A way for you to move to the edges of your comfort. Never been around grief and death? No prerequisites required.

The only thing you need is the courage to be present within your own edge. Be brave, even when you're not. This book is for you too, friend of a friend. You may not always say the right thing or have the perfect solution. But you're here and you're learning. And *that* is enough.

You Are Not Going Crazy

First thing is first ladies and gents: you are not going crazy. At whatever stage you are in the process of confronting death, no matter how totally loco things may seem right now, you are not going crazy. Yes, I know it may seem like we get very close to the edge of reality where things seem incredibly psychedelic, as if the entire world could dissipate into a thin fog and we would be left standing half-naked with a bowl of cheerios in one hand and a half-lit cigarette hanging out of our mouths wondering how this all happened.

Believe me, I've been there and I continue to go there. That edge is important. Some may call it an edge of sanity but that seems to give the illusion that there is a point you may "break" or "lose it". I'm here to tell you that you are perfectly fine just where you are. Wherever you are. If you can in the moment, take a deep breath in and say to yourself: "I'm okay. I am home. I am here. I am still breathing, and everything is as it should be."

The other thing I want you to know is that your experience is valid. Every flavor of it. The highs, and the lows. That freaky part where you're not quite sure where your hand ends and the wall begins. Where you're questioning how an experience can be *so much*. Yes, I know. I'm here for you darlings. Yes you. Mhm ... yeah honey I'm talking about Y-O-U.

My Lover, The Grim Reaper

We all approach death from different starting points. For some, it's a quick slap in the face with little to no preparation and it feels like we're standing in the middle of a field with our pants down and no first-aid kit in sight. For others, the journey to death begins long before the actual time of death is recorded, and becomes a drawn-out affair like that of an Italian opera, where yes, spoiler alert, *everyone dies*. My direct experience is of the latter (though I've had close proximity to option #1 so bear with me, folks).

My father, Richard, was a sprightly man of 62 years of age. He woke up at 5:23 am every day only because his alarm clock got stuck at that time and he chose to just go with it instead of buying a new one like a normal person. The man ran five miles every morning, followed by calisthenics, a healthy breakfast, and a short nap as he rode the train to his architecture firm in New York City. A leisurely stroll followed a light lunch and after a few more hours of work, he was off to play with his urban volleyball league.

This dude was going for the long haul. He was planning to beat out his grandmother for the longevity award, and he had a little ways to go as she died at 106. But he was totally golden. No end in sight, all systems go.

His body, however, had other ideas.

When the diagnosis of brain tumor came after two weeks of living with an impetuous drunk toddler dressed as a 6 foot 2 Texan man, it became clear this wasn't going to be a regular pony ride. We were gearing up for the quadruple loop monster coaster and all of our seat belts were slightly loose.

Terminal diagnosis. Three months to live, tops. Glioblastoma astrocytoma. He was lucky that he had the body of a 40-year-old otherwise he'd probably already be dead. The tumor is what caused the personality change, you see. A man who was normally buttoned up and reserved was now acting like a frat boy on spring break after his tenth tequila shot. All he wanted was female attention and *snacks*.

Sitting on my hippy yoga friend's living room floor after visiting Dad in the emergency room, I took a long draw of good ol' greenery from a neighborly marijuana pipe. As the mind-altering smoke filled my lungs, it became clear that I had just joined an elite club. The 'high' life indeed!

The cancer club is one with VIP access only. Once you're in, you can be sure you're in for one hell of a ride and you'll probably check a few boxes off your own bucket list too. The good news is: you're not alone! Your friends and family have guest passes too!

Here's the catch: you will not get out alive. The you that you once knew will be no more. Even your loved ones will be permanently altered by this experience like a perpetual mushroom trip but better, because *snacks*. Opportunity is knocking at your door, dear friend. This is the little gift we all came into this world carrying and yet we push it into the darkest depths of our pockets along with chewed-up bubblegum wrappers, five pennies, and that questionable-looking hair tie that seems to be growing googly eyes.

No one wants to look at this stuff and when you mention it a lot of people seem to disappear into thin air. As if it was communicable, this death sentence. Yes, you or a loved one may be dying or dead yet it cannot immediately touch those with whom you speak of it. Somehow they feel it deep within their bones. This calling. Back to the earth, to the unknown, to ... what?

Death baby, it's the name of the game. Ain't a single one of us are getting off of this earth alive.

So what's the big fuss?

ANTICIPATORY GRIEF:

Facing the Fear & Claiming the Warrior

NAME OF TOOL
Anticipatory Grief
Facing the Fear & Claiming the Warrior

BRIEF DESCRIPTION

Tune into your grief. Befriend it. It's time to reclaim your inner warrior.

CREATING SPACE

Find somewhere you won't be disturbed for 10 minutes and set your container. This could mean lighting a candle, incense, setting the tone for entering into your practice. Picturing yourself in a bubble of white light, you are fully safe, and fully protected. Tune into your IMMENSITY: the Self beyond self. All is welcome here. Once you feel fully safe, go into your fear. At your own pace. Fear of loss. Fear of the death of your loved ones. Go into it, tenderly, and slowly, and allow yourself to *feel*. *Feel* the Love on the underbelly of loss, feel the sweetness of life's passing. It's about to get very tender, beloved, so prepare yourself with water, blankets, and tissues.

PRAYER /AFFIRMATION

I am FEARLESS in my knowing that I am COURAGE embodied.
I AM strong, I AM powerful, I AM held in Divine Grace, always.
When I face my grief, I befriend it. When I lean into what scares
me, I become Whole. Through that embrace, it TRANSFORMS.
When I lean into the tenderness of Life's cycles, I get in touch with
my SOUL and my with my HEART.

A Death Dress Rehearsal

As a child, I used to lie awake at night and fantasize about the death
of my grandfather. Weird, I know. He was healthy and relatively
young for a man of 75, and I loved him dearly. I would rehearse
in my mind what it would feel like to lose him. What I would
do. I would cry and cry myself to sleep at night thinking of this.
Strangely, this was not the time he would pass (not even remotely).
Instead, he opted to leave this world a week before my father.

I think we all practice the things we most fear. What about
that man that could be around the corner as I am walking late at
night. And how about that pothole? If I hit it I could get a flat tire
and woah that would be awful! It is a sort of adaptation our brains
have made over thousands of years practicing being humans that
we have to search out the fear and potential dangers. So that we
can practice our responses. It helped for a while as we escaped the
saber tooth tiger, and we still haven't been able to shake that habit
when we sense that freaky guy standing behind us in line may have
less than noble intentions.

You can imagine my delight when I first discovered the term "anticipatory grief." It was a godsend. Finally, there was a term that described what I was feeling. That crazy-making sensation of lurking doom. No end date in sight, no time of exact relief or release from this sense of dread. I would smoke cigarettes fiendishly to sort of try and bring about this transitory state.

Like somehow I could get so nicotine-high that I would break through the veil and I would figure out what it was I was trying to understand. How and when my father would pass. My brain was trying to ascertain the danger and the correct fear response. Fight, flight, or — and here's the kicker y'all: freeze. I was frozen. There was nowhere to fly to, there was nothing to physically fight. And so I froze. I froze … staring out over the pond as I puffed my American Spirit. I gazed into the abyss. The stillness of the frozen pond. The Canadian geese traveling over the icy surface with their webbed toes. They skimmed the surface of what was lurking beneath the depths.

I don't have much to offer here aside from understanding. I know how you feel if you are anticipating the passing of a loved one. I am here for you. I know it seems interminable. It is lagging. It is drudgery. It is at times: hopelessness. But hey, we can at least have some fun with it as we go, right?

The tool here is patience. Gosh, that sounds so horrible! If only I *could* be patient, right?

The offering here is to pause and have the patience to just … be. To understand that yes, all this too can be right here, right now. You don't need to have all the answers. You don't need to have it all figured out. You don't need to do some grand gesture, or solve some huge issue or rift. You can just be, and just breathe, and just be okay. Space in the here and now. Alright? Alright.

What I am saying here is fuck the rules. On how to handle, how to grieve, how to come to terms with something both so immense and, ultimately, inspirational. How to bring that humor in as crazy-beautiful wonder-making wisdom where what you imagined you were capable of being with, living (and laughing) through, was just the tip of the iceberg. An invitation YOU had been extending to YOU since the day you were born in this cosmic whirligig of samsara. To say a tantric, insouciant, fuck Yes, to death, to this, to Spirit.

In the moments where you freeze up and panic, thinking: "there must be an end in sight! When will this all end?" — take a moment, take a deep breath (or a puff of your tobacco stick if that's your thing) and allow. Notice your surroundings. Soften into the present moment. Enjoy the journey. Yes, it can really suck at times. It can be messy, and I am here to tell you that yes, all this too is love. This too, is good and right.

All this too is what I have come to believe is "God." And I use that term to describe the unknowable, the unattainable because how can we ever possibly understand the hugeness and vastness of the creator? All that is known is that within the chaos that we can be feeling as we go through this, there is order. Out of chaos comes order. Don't worry. It will all become clear as you go. You will look back at this time with a warm fondness. You made it through. Within the pages of this book, you will find a way of dealing with it all. Even as you begin to navigate the impending passing of your beloved. It will ease the experience, I hope.

Why Me? Why Not Me?

Often I've noticed that people can tune into a sense of "why me?" That sense of victimhood. Why me? Why my loved one? Why do I have this pile of rubbish sitting at my feet and no one else to deal with it but me? I found myself sinking into that despair as well when I first heard the diagnosis for my Dad. Well, that is not entirely true. When I first heard I was strangely elated because it meant I could use it as a way to get out of work that day. Then I realized it would be a valid excuse for taking mental health days for a while to come. Gosh, go ahead and milk it, sweetie!

Truthfully, the feelings of *why me?* most definitely hit hard. In between mopey long walks listening to sad music and gazing up at the crescent autumn moon. I gazed and asked pleadingly *why me?* I was young, just bursting into my early 20's. I wanted to be a funny girl. A famous comedienne. How was I supposed to make light of this? Perhaps more unselfishly, I thought *why us?* Why my family? A family that had already been ripped apart at the roots. A family still reeling from the abandonment and loss of our extended family. A family who'd spent countless thanksgivings and Christmases painfully trying to recreate a sense of cohesion after the heartbreak. After the accusation that my father had molested my cousin — an accusation from a repressed memory never proved — and now this? Would we ever know if he truly was guilty of the crime of which he was accused? What was it like for him not having an outlet to talk to anyone about it?

Why him? He had spent his whole life quietly trying to live each day with a semblance of normalcy.

Producing a painted picture convincing the world "we're okay." When the truth was that for many years we were in hell.

Mia, my older sister, had been wracked with a violent depression. Then, an even more devastating dive into anorexia that nearly killed her. And my mother. Forever holding the weight of the loss of her mother, father, sisters, nieces and nephews on her shoulders. On her belly, waist, thighs. She ate to numb the feeling of loss.

Why us? I'd spent years trying to feel as if I was worthy enough to actually present myself to the world. Attempting to shed beliefs of unlovable-ness. I wanted to show I was successful. Pretty enough, smart enough, courageous enough. To the family who had failed to love me, I wanted to be a wild show of success. To get there I starved myself, I binged and purged. I snapped rubber bands on my wrists to quell feelings of hunger. A slow torture into a planned view of perceived perfection. Always out of my grasp. Never able to attain.

Why me? Why this? Hadn't we suffered enough? After years of trying to just get our heads barely above the water then came this blow. This diagnosis. So sure, I spent some incredible time wallowing in the depths of self-pity. The *why me?* is a tempting mistress. She tells us to just take another break. You're a delicate flower. You don't deserve this. It propels us into feelings of victimhood. I had spent enough years of my life feeling like a victim. *Enough.*

So this is where we Pause, get really still, and whisper to ourselves: "*why not me*"? What makes you/me so special that you would be excused from having this sort of experience? It is a strange salvation to come to terms with this understanding. Why not me? Can I handle this? I am a strong motherlickah and I think by golly I was made for this journey. I was made to crush this b*tch. Yeah! I can do it, why not? Why *not* me?

You know how some people really resent the phrase "God only gives us what we can handle"? Not me, sister. I relish it. I roll around with it and luxuriate in it, like I was laying naked on animal fur in front of a mansion's stone fireplace. Yes darling, this too, you purr. This too is all yours. So instead of sitting around moping (and sure, you're free to do that too) ... when you're not busy feeling sorry for yourself, why not pour yourself a tonic and offer your words to the heavens? Embrace it all.

Yes, all this too.

And why *not* Me?

This is the opportunity to embrace the Why Not Me mentality. What is it about this that scares you? How can you bend and break yourself into that something new that you are becoming? My advice here is twofold. First: do something that absolutely makes you sh*t your pants. Totally out of the ordinary for you. Something to shock you out of swimming in the stages of fight/flight/freeze response. Go skydiving, learn macrame, sign up to perform at an open mic night, take an ice skating lesson, text your crush! The second is to do something with this time in between if your loved one has yet to pass.

Pre-death Pro Tips from a Death Doula

Be proactive and prepare for the inevitable. Getting this sh*t in order will save you headaches, heartaches, and more.

Legacy:

- How does your loved one want to be remembered? What mythology do they want to leave behind?
- Ideas: record audio of them telling their stories, work on writing an obituary with them, note down all their prized possessions

Get their affairs in order:

- Have their Will arranged and signed with a lawyer
- Review their Advance Care Directives (Download forms by State at AARP online, these legally binding forms allow patients to designate who makes health care decisions for them in the event that they are unable to voice their wishes)

It records their wishes specifically including:

- Who their health proxy is (their appointed medical decision-maker)
- When/when not to resuscitate
- Options for life-sustaining treatment
- Organ donation
- Pain relief
- Funeral planning

Secure all social media, e-mail, computer passwords:

- Many platforms allow for a proxy to take over if pre-arranged

Secure access to all important documents including:

- Social security card
- Birth certificate
- Passport
- Medical records

Understandably it can be incredibly difficult to have these conversations before a loved one passes. Although the anguish that comes if not properly planned beforehand can outweigh the emotional pain of facing it head-on. A stitch in time, y'all. Approach it kindly and carefully.

Death Cleaning

Death Cleaning is the process of going through your loved one's things. It's a great way to prepare (and keep yourself busy) and entails gently beginning to go through their belongings. Find out what is super important to them. Their clothes, their high school diploma, photographs, that strange jar of unidentifiable food things? Yep — your loved one lived a whole life! And as they say when you die: "You can't take it with you!"

A great way to prepare (and keep yourself busy) is to gently begin going through their belongings. Find out what is super important to them. What do they want to pass down to their grandchildren? This is a big process and there are great tools out there for getting this done before their passing. A favorite resource is: *The Gentle Art of Swedish Death Cleaning* by Margareta Magnusson, which walks through how to get a space ready for a person to leave it. My favorite book while cleaning out my Dad's things and my grandparent's house was Marie Kondo's *The Life-Changing Magic of Tidying Up: the Japanese Art of Decluttering and Organizing*.

Her book really helped me tune into each object, notice whether it brought me joy and gave me the courage to release what no longer served. Try it out. I know it is a big bite to chew off, but you can do it. Remember, there are also professionals who can help you do this! You don't have to do it alone. You can even invite a friend over to hang as you sift through boxes. It takes a village.

What to Anticipate & Common Misconceptions

When caring for a loved one in the process of their passing we often have the very human urge to care for them as we would any other unwell person. Our instincts tell us they need to eat more food, drink water, get up and moving, lift their spirits! This is where we have to unlearn all that we think comes naturally to healing. The issue here is that the person is not going to get well. It is absolutely heartbreaking to admit, don't get me wrong.

One of the biggest takeaways I brought with me is the knowledge that when a person is dying, the most important thing you can do is *allow them to show the way*. Often a person will refuse food and drink. Do not force this. The body is an extremely intelligent creature and knows how it wants to go. In distress, we may plead with them to please just take one sip! The heartbreaking reality is that this actually lengthens and prolongs the dying process.

We must not force someone to eat when they know instinctively that they have no need for nourishment as they prepare to travel into the great beyond. Food is life-sustaining. So when we force it upon our dearly departing beloveds we must pause and reflect. Is this perhaps a selfish longing? Do we do this because we really just want them to stick around a little while longer? I don't blame you, certainly not.

But know that the greatest gift you can give them is to use what we call in Improv the "Yes, and" practice. Instead of telling them that their needs are invalid such as "why do you want the window open, it is the middle of winter you'll freeze to death!" or "come on, just get out of bed and socialize a little" or "just take three bites, you'll feel better!" — the option here is to ask them: "What do you need?"

It may sound crazy whatever it is they want. Of course. But the key here is to *trust* that their soul is preparing the best way it knows how to make this grand journey. When your loved one exclaims out loud "my grandmommy is here!" when you see no living soul in the room with you, instead of correcting them: use the "Yes, and". Try: "Yes, and isn't it wonderful she came!"

We're not here to tell them how to die. We're here to support them as they make this courageous leap. So instead of putting what you believe is best for them at the forefront, let them lead the way.

It's also helpful to know the distinction between dying and active dying. Often the hospice nurses will help you distinguish when this begins. People differ though the general guide is that a person will begin to enter active dying within 7-14 days before their passing. You'll begin to notice marked shifts in their demeanor.

- **They turn inward, are less out-wardly focused**
- **A far-away look is in their eyes, inability to focus**
- **Less communicative**
- **Decreased interest in foods and liquids (a sponge swab can be used to keep the mouth moist for comfort)**
- **Slowed breathing**
- **Decreased urine output, urine is a dark tea-colored brown**
- **Visions/Hallucinations**
- **Potentially entering into a coma**
- **Audible death rattle**

I'd always imagined the death rattle was this huge booming sound that happened at the moment of death. I'd asked people about it and all they said was "oh it was awful, this loud sound, I couldn't stand it!" but they never shared more. In my mind I imagined a menacing-looking grim reaper holding a rattle and shaking it like a loud rattlesnake. While my Dad was in the earlier stages of hospice I went deep into my research. Determined to get to the bottom of it, I scoured YouTube for real-life videos of what the sound was like. Thank goodness for the internet, guys. And thank goodness for YouTube. Great for home improvement tutorials, and this. I found out that the death rattle was not a huge instant booming noise though rather more of a slow trickle of a sound.

The best way most people characterize it is that it sounds like percolating coffee. Like a low and persistent gurgle. Often family members will think it is causing the person discomfort though this is a misconception. It causes them no pain and it simply occurs when the patient loses their ability to clear their throat and saliva and mucus builds up in the back of their throats causing this gurgling, coffee-maker-like sound. You may never look at coffee the same way, but rest assured, your loved one is naturally progressing through their active dying phase. All is well just be with them and allow.

General Tips on Caring For the Actively Dying

Why waste flowers by sending them after they've died? Go the beauty way and make their dying space magnificent!

Make them comfortable with options for:

- **Blankets**
- **Fans**
- **Humidifiers**
- **Aromatherapy (smell can be amplified during dying so use when welcomed)**
- **Soothing music**
- **Ambiance: candles, flowers**

Grieving the Loss of Anticipated "Guaranteed Experiences"

When losing a loved one we also have to contend with the reality that they just won't "be there" for some of the most important moments in our lives. This is a tough reality to face for many. What I find helpful is to really relish and swim in these deep feelings. It is a way of mourning that which will never be. Allow the sorrow to live and breathe there. What is it that you always counted on happening and looked forward to, maybe not even actively? For me, it was realizing my father would never be around to walk me down the aisle at my wedding. Not being much of the type of girl to fantasize about this, it was strange for me to suddenly mourn the loss of something I hadn't given much thought to until the moment it was taken away from me.

The new realities that come and go since he has been gone continue to surprise me. Moving into a new home, meeting a new partner, doing a home renovation, small victories in my career. All things we will not get to experience with them by our side. Often when these things come up I allow space for them. There's a reason it is here to teach me. It is an opportunity to connect more deeply to who they were. To honor and cherish them. Mourn them, yes. But also it draws light onto all the things I loved about them.

So while they won't be around to hold the small body of my firstborn child, or congratulate me on the next big business win, or heck even the release of this book! I know I can hold space for that. Take time out and do my grieving practices. Go to a power place. Cry, dance, sing, drum it out. To acknowledge the moments never yet to come. Yes, all this too.

Journaling Practice:

- **Make a list of all the "guaranteed experiences" your loved one will miss**
- **What would they love most about being there with you?**
- **What would they say to you? Any words of advice?**
- **What would they wear for the occasion?**
- **How would it feel to have them with you?**

Post Loss: Anticipating Death-iversaries

This is gonna suck. I will not lie to you. Not only will the death anniversary of your loved one suck, oh no. There are just SO many more dates that will be absolutely gut-wrenching. Why sugarcoat it? I'm giving you fair warning now so you can be prepared. Tell your boss you'll need the full week off, if not the whole month. The birthdays, the holidays, *your* birthday, their special day that celebrates who they were, "Happy Mother's Day," etc. Those hallmark holidays. Valentine's day when your loved one would always send a box of sweets when you were alone drinking wine with your cat. Those little days that meant so much to you when they were around. Those are gonna be shitty. So super duper crappy. Okay?

Let yourself do it up right. Get your time off to work through the emotions as they arise. And hey, here is the crazy part: you'll think you're doing fine. You're cruising along on your grief path and you're fine and dandy then *bam* it hits you like a ton of bricks. Shoot, you look at the calendar — *that* day is coming up soon. "Surely, I can ignore it" you say. Think again! If you don't get yourself set up to absolutely shred this upcoming day beforehand, it will absolutely annihilate you when it arrives.

So, learn from a pro, okay? Take some time off, book yourself a few therapy sessions, a massage, a mani-pedi. Stock up on all your fave snacks and make sure you've got your homies on speed dial. Heck, let them know ahead of time and maybe even plan for a few to come sleep over and make tent forts in your living room to cry in. You know the ones. The down for anything, ride-or-die friends. They will come through and help. Because we can get through this. And Yes, all this too. The passing of a loved one is a gift that keeps on giving. Like the surprise party you never knew you wanted and then it is here, and all this is such magic you can't help but love it all completely.

The good news: I guarantee it gets easier as each year passes. Trust. It may never leave, though it will change with time. With the right tools, you'll anticipate the coming day and rock like the Grief warrior you are!

Grief-tivities to do on Anniversaries and Shitty Hallmark Holidays:

- **Stock up on snacks and beverages (or snax and bevvies as I call them)**
- **Cook your loved one's fave meal, set an extra plate just for them (ancestor plate)**
- **Do that one thing they loved to do (fly fishing, puppeteering, model airplane flying)**
- **Pull out their favorite craft. MahJong? Scrap booking? Crochet?**
- **Buy their fave beer or wine, and drink it with a friend and pour some on the earth as an offering**
- **Go on a long hike, find an epic power place and scream high into the heavens — YODEL!**
- **Rearrange your ancestor altar: put out fresh photos, their favorite drink, candies, etc**
- **Throw on a shamanic journeying track, lay down, and ask them to come through and offer their lessons**
- **Get your hair done, just because: we can look good while we're grieving can't we?**
- **Post pix on your social media of them: gone but not forgotten**

- **Blast their favorite musical. Even if you hate it. Carousel anybody?**
- **Pick up the instrument they loved to play, blast their top jams and rock it out**

BEWARE OF THE VULTURES:

It's About Boundaries, Baby

NAME OF TOOL
Beware of the Vultures
It's About Boundaries, Baby

BRIEF DESCRIPTION

Boundaries are essential. Both internal and external. They will hold you, and they will revitalize you.

SET THE CONTAINER

Find somewhere where you won't be disturbed for 5 minutes and set your container. This could mean lighting a candle, incense, setting the tone for entering into practice. If you've got mad creative visualization skills, hell yes, you can do this anytime and anywhere. The only limit is your faith. In your mind's eye, picture a pink egg of energy all around you. Is it a mesh of feathers? A chain mail like-substance that doesn't allow anything or anyone is not in the highest good in? Feel into it and create a barrier that allows you to repel anyone or anything not in your highest good.

PRAYER/AFFIRMATION

I AM held in a bubble of light and love. I easily release anything that isn't mine. I move forward with clear energy into the effervescent now.

"OMG I'm so sorry to hear about your Dad's cancer! You should totally join this upcoming 5k run for the charity I'm organizing!"... squeal.

Ho-ly sh*t. I cannot with this. I tried, and I simply cannot. I have to tell you something super important okay? Do NOT run that 5k for charity your random acquaintance tells you about in passing. If you really want to, go for it, but do not do it if they are begging you to do something that *they* think is gonna be "totally great" for you and your healing. This comes from personal experience, y'all. A few days after my Dad's diagnosis, a bouncy mom from my Long Island yoga studio approached me after a class. She wanted me to join this race their friend had organized for a random charity that she felt was semi-related to my father's illness. And no, I did not go.

I could not even handle the fact that I was now facing a potentially long and painful path of grief and healing and more pain. I was a recent inductee to the cancer club. I could not even fathom joining a 5k race for anything. People will offer things to you like this. They believe they are trying to "help" and have no idea how their "kind" words are falling on deaf ears. Ain't nobody wanna join a 5k when they're in the depths of this s-h-i-t. Unless this is you, and again, go for it. I am not here to take the wind out of your sails. I simply think it should be something you do, for YOU, and not anyone else.

So this brings up the important topic of vultures. You know the kind? Nasty looking black birds that circle above a recently deceased animal carcass. They're visible for miles. Swarming around the dead thing and they can't help themselves, this is what they do. It is their "thing." We can't take it personally and we certainly can't let it in once we understand what they are. The thing about grief, death, dying is that these same sorts of creatures will gather around you but you won't immediately recognize them. It will come to you by way of your friendly neighbor, or a kind acquaintance you have through a mutual friend who happens to know so-and-so. Many people will gather around your pain. It is okay. Some are genuine angels and it is your job to discern them. It is your job to know your boundaries. Maintain your boundaries, okay? It will come as a bit of a surprise — they sit you down and ask you a few questions about your loved one. You can offer what feels comfortable, then if they begin into a lengthy talk about their distant friend or relative they knew that also had cancer and "oh gosh it was so horrible for them, the radiation, the chemo, the tubes, the hospitalizations, and yes they died a very catastrophic death, but I'm sure it isn't the same for your loved one!"

Then they're gone. They're off circling over-head and stewing in their own pain, their own grief. Their own story. Occasionally it may be helpful, though you can't always be sure. If someone corners you and begins telling you a story about their so-and-so, feel free to cut them right off. You can offer a "thank you so much, and I am really not in a place to receive this right now". Then walk the fuq away!

People use your pain as a way to work on their own. It is understandable. And yes, as I said, occasionally it can be helpful though be careful who you let in. Be extra discerning. They may work their way into your world so deeply that it slowly becomes more about them than about your pain. I had people hijack a friendly conversation about my Dad's recent therapies into a long ass story about their passed brother who had died of brain cancer over 20 years earlier. Old news! Can't with that! Nope nope nope. Do not pass go. Do not collect $200.

It is rarely helpful when they are reliving their trauma and pain. I know this may sound cut-throat. It is. Do not engage. Walk away and do not look back. If you have a friend you trust who has a similar story and you know they will be able to be present for your journey, yes, of course, go for it. But screen them carefully. This is your time. Go ahead, be selfish.

Sorry your Dog Died, Now Get Lost!

Three months after my Dad died I was in Bali on my Griefcation®. It was a magical time where I met many beings who helped me on my journey. The community of ex-pats who live there full-time are varied and wild. They come from all around the world and offer creative ways of wearing your class of wisdom.

I was sitting in a hot tub in a place called Dragonfly Village, after a group of us had been singing in rounds in a Turkish hammam. Across from me was an older woman I had become acquainted with. She'd lived in Bali for a number of years and was a mainstay in the spiritual community there. I had been feeling very lonely and needing someone to talk to about what I was going through. Bali is filled with healers and people of all sorts coming to help others on their journeys. So I was delighted to hear she had worked as a therapist in her career before coming to live as a retired expat. She looked like an older Judy Garland sitting across from me in the warm water. I decided to open up to her with hopes that she would take me on as a client. Perhaps a bit unorthodox, but Bali can be like that. I told her about the passing of my father a few months before. Her eyes lit up. I was excited to hear her reply.

"Oh! I am so glad you reminded me of this. I can't believe it. I am just now remembering my beloved dog I lost a few years ago. Oh my goodness, it was heart wrenching. In the end it was really so sad, you know. He was 60 pounds and he couldn't walk. Even to go to the bathroom I had to help him by lifting his legs. Oh my goodness, it was so hard, you have really touched me by reminding me of my dog." Her eyes were filled with tears.

I knew at that moment this woman had nothing to give me. In fact I was enraged. In her selfishness, she went on this long monologue about her damn dog (and don't get me wrong I know the love of animals and how hard it is to lose them) but jesus-effing-christ. This was not the time to talk about the dang dog! There is a difference between a dog and a human! I was so angry because only months before then I had been changing the diapers of a man who was immobile, six-foot-two, and almost three hundred pounds. I didn't feel safe telling her this. I promptly exited the hot tub and drove myself home through the jungle on my moped moodily smoking a clove cigarette. It wasn't meant to be. And that was okay.

Boundaries Are Your Friend. This is the medicine. Make your own space so that it is *impenetrable*. So that the outside influences of others' energy cannot come in if they are not within the highest integrity and intention. You don't need that anymore! You have enough on your plate. It will all ease up eventually and you can relax. You can trust to talk with people about it again at a time in the future. But when you are really in your grief, and in your process, protect your energy. Protect your story. If you sense a vulture overhead, heed the call to cover yourself in the safe bounds of your inner power.

Oh Sh*t! The Veil is Open!

When I first experienced my awakening sh*t was freaking wild. What started off as a sort of playful dalliance into the field of Spirit soon turned into something wildly uncontrollable. At first, I would see spirits during my walks at night. I would feel someone whispering into my ears as I fell asleep at night. I would feel the presence of great beings, angels and ancestors surrounding me. A warm hug or a tap on the shoulder when I was all alone. Then it changed into seeing lights around me, like little fairies. Or seeing energy both golden and dark. Like small fragments of beings flashing out of the corner of my eye.

After my ayahuasca ceremonies, I was completely and totally blasted open. I call it "popping the top off". There was literally no veil between me and the spirit world and I was in full connection 24/7. I couldn't walk down the street because I would look into someone's eyes and see everything about them. Their lives, their ancestors, the spirits surrounding them wanting to communicate. I would see their pain, the hang ups, their hopes and dreams. Memories of theirs. It was like being an open antenna for spirit like a radio station tuned into every freaking station.

When riding the subway I would feel the thoughts and feel-ings of every person sitting or standing around me. Talk about a cacophony! In conversations, I would somehow already know the entire sequence of events beforehand. I knew the arch of the conversation, what each person would say before they said it. I would know how the dialogue would conclude. Therefore I became almost like a mute. There was no reason to add anything into any conversation because I already knew the whole thing front to back. I knew people's motives, and why they said what they did. Trying to bolster themselves, impress others, defend themselves, prove their wit. I could see it all. And so I became like a little wallflower. As a lifelong extrovert, this was tough.

Standing in social circles I was just vibrating at this strange level where I could not have a normal conversation. Looking into a friend's safe eyes I would penetrate deeply into them without any permission or control. My eyelids fluttered rapidly and I would feel their entire being. It wasn't manageable or sustainable. The only way I could avoid it was to stay inside and go into deep meditations.

I learned the tools of creating my own energetic boundaries by seeking stillness. From finding small moments in my day to connect. Spirit wanted to come through and speak to me but I was not creating a safe container to do so. Instead, it was just coming in with all valves open. I needed to create a valve. I continue every day to create these valves and learn this lesson over and over again. Otherwise, I would go about my day and even if I had mostly tamped down a few of the valves, inevitably something would come in and I would have to stop everything and let it come through. Like a download of energy. Sometimes filled with words and others like an energetic upgrade I would feel this molten-like energy flowing into my brain.

Every morning I now create a container, connect, and put on my spiritual seat belt. I create time to go inwards and receive what it was spirit needs to communicate to me. Like finely tuning the radio station so that it is receiving only what is for my highest good. How do I do this? Releasing tension from my body. Learning to fully relax into a seated sitting posture, aligning my energy centers, learning how to create containers, and to show up for them, to self-heal.

A great way to shore up your energetic boundaries is taking Ritual Baths. Fill up your tub with warm water. And fill with a large scoop of Himalayan salt or Epsom salts. You can feel free to customize depending on your vibe. Maybe add a couple of drops of lavender essential oils. Maybe you dry skin brush beforehand then cover your body in sesame oil before lowering yourself into your ritual waters. Make the space sacred by lighting candles. Set the mood with relaxing music. One of my favorite places to release sound with my voice. Not only a great way to release deep emotions but also wonderful for protecting your energetic sphere. The salt acts as a neutralizer. It transmutes negative juju and builds a force field around you.

My favorite tool for getting messages has been Shamanic journeying. I will take 15-30 minutes a day, light a candle, smudge my space, and listen to a shamanic journeying track. Sometimes I will drum or rattle myself. Then I go into my meeting place within the spirit realm. I meet with my main spirit animal boo thang. We hang for a moment, reconnect, I will sometimes adorn them with jewels, necklaces, or golden salves. Then we are off. They either carry me on their back as we run through the world or we fly, swim, whatever the journey needs.

I usually have an intention as I go in. What do I need clarity on? What do I want to know? What spirit guides do I need to connect with? What healing do I or a loved one need? What healing does the earth need? Then as I journey I meet with other beings and learn from the visions what it is I must do. I gain the tools I need, the methods of healing, or the wisdom. This has been my main tool for allowing this energy to have an access point in my practice.

Many people find their own, I encourage you to do the same. Some people love free writing and channeling. Some just love simple stillness, a mindful meditation. If your veil is totally thin and the top is completely popped the heck off, it helps to find practices that ground in the experience. We put on our spiritual seat belts in the morning and in the evening we take them off. This prepares us for our days so that we can be balanced and centered individuals in society. Surround yourself each morning and evening in a bubble of pink, healing, loving light. A center of presence that guides you. Nothing can penetrate this bubble without your permission.

A tip from a friend: leave a flower outside the bubble so if someone or something wants to get near it, they can come up to the flower, then you can decide if you allow it in. You are the one in control here. If you're just starting out I highly recommend finding a group of people to help you learn more. Whether it is a meditation circle, or a shamanic journeying group. Whatever it is that you feel most called to. We can find like minded individuals who may also be experiencing a thin veil. We can learn how to protect ourselves and feel less alone when we have a spiritual community around us.

All of this takes a strange sense of courage. A willingness to dive into the deep end. An eagerness to know thyself. And to unknow yourself. To allow the old to dissolve and gain new tools of empowerment. To have the courage to see your newly birthed self as whole. Holy. Armed and ready. Impervious to outside entities and distractions. You are fully manned within. You have gone through the death of the ego. You have dissolved what you once were. Attachments to old identities. Because as we go through this thing called grief, we become forever changed. We cannot hold on to the old self so we find ways of easing it as it dissolves. Of connecting to that small whisper within that we can trust. A whisper that says: yes. you're ready.

CEMETERY CHIC:

How to Put the 'Fun' in "Funeral"

NAME OF THE TOOL
Cemetery Chic
How to Put the 'Fun' in "Funeral"

BRIEF DESCRIPTION

Adorn Yourself, Radiant One! It's nourishing in ways you may not imagine.

SET THE CONTAINER

Go to your local thrift shop and put yourself on a $50 budget. Then go to freakin town. And /or: have a besties clothing swap party! Or, if luxury is calling your name ... have at it. One life to live. Treat yourself to the medicine of adornment. Cloak your body in clothes, fragrances, and textures that protect and inspire you.

PRAYER /AFFIRMATION

As I adorn my body, I come home. I remember that this space is a temple that can hold all of me. I am safe to love myself. I embrace my totality.

"At every occasion, I'll be ready for the funeral
At every occasion, once more, it's called the funeral
At every occasion, oh, I'm ready for the funeral
At every occasion, oh, one billion day funeral"
"The Funeral" Band of Horses

Here's the good news: this is your grief and you're allowed to wear whatever the heck you want. This is your party and you'll cry if you want to, cry if you want to. Okay?

Ever heard the phrase "stressed but well dressed"? This is you now. Only you get to define whatever "well dressed" means. The joy of grief is that in my book, literally, anything goes. This means that if you wake up and manage to get out of bed, the world is your oyster and you are permitted to wear whatever pleases you. This applies to your day-to-day grief look as well as what you choose to wear to your loved one's funeral.

Listen, I want to impart on you a bit of my crazy wisdom. The wisdom I gained through my own runway walk through the fires of griefly hell. And by hell we mean really it was technicolor and grey and sparkly and glittered with ash. Okay that got dark. Here we go.

Warrior Hair

When Dad went into hospice, I was having a hard time showering, brushing my teeth, brushing my hair ... the bare minimum was seemingly impossible to me. I would look in the mirror and see someone with a sallow and grey face. Someone who wasn't sure what was up or down. Someone who only wanted to wear the same oversized navy blue college sweatshirt, black yoga tights, and beaded black moccasins with leg warmers. It was, in a word, a LEWK. In a way it was lovely, in its own strange way. And as I looked in the mirror I thought, I needed something else. A bit of edge.

So I called up my friend Raphael and told him I was coming over for a hair makeover. I had decided the edge I needed was "Warrior Hair". I wanted my mane to reflect the strength and courage I needed in navigating these waters. I wanted to look like an unruly beast conquering the underworld. I wanted my hair to channel the vibes of Goddess Kali Ma, who's snarled tongue and wild eyes were fantastically complemented by a wild mane. I wanted to be a medusa. Snakes slithering from my scalp. Terrifying any living man who dared cross me. I wanted to be able to stare death down and it make it my b*tch. Hair is a powerful thing.

At the time my hair was shoulder length, curly, brown, and voluminous (thank you hair gods). Raphael took me to a hair mecca shop where they sell all types of personalities through wigs, extensions, hair dye, you name it. I told Raphael of my vision as we navigated the colorful aisles of hair. We made our selection and he got to work as we smoked spliffs and listened to his band's new album. Pure magic. The hair was underway. He tugged and braided for hours. Applying layers of false hair and gems. I was in awe. Finally the moment of truth came and he spun me around to face my newly warrior-ified reflection. I was complete.

Atop my head sat a finely woven selection of colorful, woven hair wraps. Purple, red, blue, and white. Each bedazzled with sparkly gems. And one single wrap had tied to the end of it: a single compass totem. Thankful, and a bit blitzed, I went on my way. Now I had the power of these magical threads woven into my scalp. Wow. What a blessing.

Monkey Scarf

One day my mother had to sit my sister and I down for a serious discussion regarding my Dad's cancer treatment. We planned to go out to a fancy sushi restaurant in my hometown. The kind people take dates to and get dressed up for. I was feeling feisty, a bit out of sorts, and a bit "IDGAF". The desperation of the moment cued me to do something wild. Something strange. It felt right in the moment. I grabbed the stuffed spider monkey toy I'd bought on a middle school field trip to the Bronx Zoo. I'd named him Sanka after the funny character in *Cool Runnings*. I loved the character's easy going rastafarian lifestyle. He was steadfast and shatterproof. When his Jamaican Bobsled team got into a crash, his captain would ask: "Sanka, ya dead?" to which he'd wearily reply: "Yah man".

I needed Sanka's magic. His strength. His sense of humor. His hands and feet velcroed together so I could wrap him around me like a scarf. So silly. So strange. But there I was, protected by my primate friend. Hair adorned, threaded, colorful and wild. I felt downright Puckish! However bizarre it was, I didn't feel it. I had my defense going into battle. I didn't know what my mother would tell us, and now it didn't matter. For me, it worked.

Luckily, my mom and sister didn't seem to mind ... and neither did the waitress.

California roll, anyone?

The Funeral Dress

"Have you decided what you're wearing to the service yet?" my mother repeated impatiently in the days leading up to my father's funeral. I had not. I didn't want to think about it. I did not want to look into my closet (and scrounge up some old frock I had worn out to "da club" no doubt) to wear as we sent off my dear ol' Dad. The truth was, I had only been to two funerals before this and both had been for people I was not particularly close with. Not that it matters, I just want you to know I had no real experience in the "what to wear to a funeral" area of expertise.

We had lived through three years of practicing for this day and now here it was. I had been getting ready to get ready for this funeral. Playing it over in my mind for months. I had imagined all sorts of scenarios. Showing up in a white cape atop a noble steed, with a boombox perched on my shoulder blasting "Screw you, we're from Texas" by Ray Wylie Hubbard. That would have been cool. And no, no, that didn't seem quite right. Not that I cared what the neighbors thought but, I had to be mildly sensible, I knew this at least.

Off to Mystique Boutique, a local bargain shopping place where all the designs were crafted for those most definitely heading to "da club". I liked this store because it was unpretentious and you could put together a decent looking outfit for under $25. Most of the frocks I'd try on seemed to be cut out with scissors by a toddler. Half a tittie exposed here, a butt cheek hanging out there. This shop wasn't exactly respectable. But with a good eye, one could put together something truly remarkable. I navigated the racks with the eyes of a laser sharp shark, on the hunt for my prey. I found a somber (yet sexy) woven, black turtleneck dress. Hot. Tres chic. This thing could be wheeled around Paris and have all les mecs saying: "ooh la la!" Although there was something missing. A certain "Je ne sais quoi". And then, I saw it.

In the corner of the store was something so strange, so horrible, so totally out there that it had me thinking: "who would possibly wear this thing?" And that was when I realized that yes ... it was me. I would be the one donning this black and white striped faux fur knee length vest. This thing looked like it got lost somewhere between a Prada runway and a burning man drug den. It was wild. It was out there. It was perfect.

The Yellow Rose of Texas

So the day finally came. We'd ordered 300 yellow roses from Columbia. On sale, somehow. We joked the roses were so cheap because they were shipped with smuggled cocaine so you'd get a little hit when you took a whiff. The room was set, completely packed. Standing room only. Filled with the wonderful souls my father had known on his earthly walk.

And then there I was. Walking down the church aisle like a goddamn queen. Red heels. Red lips. Giant black sunglasses. My chic as fuq black turtleneck dress, and draped in this horri-fabulous faux fur and my wild warrior hair. It was SO inappropriate, and altogether perfect at the same time. Since Dad had been a rock star in his earlier days, this was my ode to his inner child of rock n' roll.

Because in moments like these, it's your party and you'll look fly if you want to.

Crying in Public: A How-to-Guide

Water will come to cleanse you, at exactly the time it is meant to. Sometimes this feels inconvenient because our culture struggles with grief, with intense emotion. With feeling things fully, as they come. Grieving in the city gave me some good strategies as far as how to be in public with grief.

- **Find a good pair of sunglasses**
- **Wear a fabulous hood or scarf**
- **Headphones/music optional**
- **Find a small corner, place to sit, or walk on a busy city street**
- **Open the flood gates**

DEATH AS A SPIRITUAL PRACTICE:

Today is a Good Day to Die

NAME OF THE TOOL
Death as a Spiritual Practice
Today is a Good Day to Die

BRIEF DESCRIPTION

It's time to befriend the benevolent darkness. By practicing emptiness, you merge with the holy void.

SET THE CONTAINER

Find somewhere where you won't be disturbed for 5 minutes and set your container. Whatever that means for you. Some examples could be lighting a candle, incense, setting the tone for entering into practice. In this space, enter in the silence and let yourself embrace the unknown. As you enter the meditation, ask yourself: Who am I really? Keep asking this question. Expand your perceptions to include all beings. The whole planet. Nature. And further up to include space, our galaxy, and further ... to become the blackness, the void, itself.

PRAYER /AFFIRMATION

I awaken to a deeper practice of silence, letting go of all identifications. I gently surrender to the void, so that the void may reveal its true treasures.

The French speak of an orgasm as a "little death" or "le petite mort" which is what I think death is really all about. A sublime merging with bliss. The ultimate reality. The peace that surpasses all understanding.

We live in a death-phobic culture. A place where these things are hushed up and brushed under the rug, and "oh dear, we don't talk about those things at the dinner table, darling". I am here to say "fuq that!" to all of it. Death to me is an ultimate taboo. A strange sense of kink that I want to sit in and make love to. No, not in *that* way, ya freak.

I think death offers us a place of meeting ourselves. As we sit and contemplate it, we invite in an inner journey that brings us deeper into our own subconscious, our own traumas, shadow selves, inner longings, and fears. I want to pull the wool off of all our eyes in this death phobic culture and begin to stare deeply into the void-like beyond that is death. The limitlessness. The Who knows what? Yes. To me death is both a mystery and: a practice.

How can we invite death into our lives as a spiritual practice? It begins with your invitation.

Have a Cup o' Tea with Death

Step one in beginning your death as a spiritual practice is acknowledging that you've come to this place. You're here, you're eager, and all you have to do is ask. Do you remember a moment when death first came knocking? I do.

I was laying on my bed in the basement of my parent's Long Island home. It was the evening of December 21st, 2012, a date I had long feared. As a high school freshman, our social studies teacher had shown us a terrifying video telling us that according to the Mayan Prophecy, the world would end on that very date. BLAST! KABLAMO! OBLIVION! Honestly the lack of forethought these teachers had in showing this to a traumatized group of youths who experienced 9/11 first hand only a few short years earlier is astounding in hindsight. We had all experienced the terror. Not hearing from our parents working in the city that day. We saw the large cloud of smoke rising high over the cold blue autumn waters of our hometown. We walked through the streets in the following days smelling a scent unlike any other I've been able to place since. It was death. In the air. The grit of death in our nostrils. We felt it and as children, we could feel what we did not understand.

This led to a wild cascade of fears that enveloped me for years. The fear of impending doom. Of an end I could not prevent, but one that would be cataclysmic and final. I would sit in my high school math class and stare out the window at the school buses arriving in the courtyard outside. I'd imagine huge fireballs crashing down and demolishing all in sight. It was no wonder I failed my math classes miserably. I blame it all on this damn prophecy.

In the months leading up to the fateful date, I'd become increasingly involved with the Brooklyn spiritual scene. I was 22 at the time and eager to find a meaning beyond all the misery that is your early 20's. What was going on here? I could sense something was shifting though I did not know what. In these groups I felt a sense of community. We'd dance together wildly in strange Brooklyn warehouses, with psychedelic art projected onto the walls and ceilings. I was sober, aside from a hint of marijuana. Lost in the dreaming. I dreamt of an awakening rather than an ending of days like the Mayans had predicted. I had begun to grow hopeful.

Since Dad's diagnosis, I had become more aware already. New abilities began opening up to me in ways I did not understand. I found a dusty old book of my father's from the 70's on ESP a.k.a Extra Sensory Perception. This seemed to fit in with a lot of what I was experiencing. I began to sense things that I could not explain though felt palpably and had a sense of inner knowing of the truth.

I lay awake as the clock moved closer towards midnight on the night of December 21st, 2012. Softly accepting my fate while silently bracing for anything. In the room above me I sensed my father sleeping on the pull-out couch next to my mom. He was fresh out of his first brain surgery. His head shaved and adorned with a long stretch of black-blood-caked staples holding together his skull. He was alive though just barely. Shaken. Torn from the extremely health conscious life he led a mere months before.

As I laid in bed I felt a sense of something wash over me. It felt like a cold dark blanket. A silent observer. It had consciousness though not of life. It was not evil, or mean. Rather neutral and steady. Bold and solidly present. I knew instinctively this was death. Then all of a sudden I heard a rattling sound from the boiler room next to my bed. "Oh no," I thought, "this is it. This is the reckoning the Mayans spoke about!" I squeezed my eyes shut and braced for impact. It will soon be over. And I waited. And then the noise began again. A sort of agitated shuffling about. What could this be?

I was terrified.

I waited a few more moments, curled up in bed with the blankets clenched tightly around my neck. Til—again—the rattling persisted.

Sensing something was at hand I slowly began to peel myself away from my bed. Tip-toeing toward the door I slowly grabbed the handle and cracked it open to peek my head into the dark, musty room. This was the only unfinished room in the basement and if there was ever a place to find something spooky, this was it. Old shelves full of discarded baby toys covered in dust, an antique mac computer, a deteriorating brown leather bag, white cardboard file boxes. A single string hung from above to switch on the stand alone light bulb. I pulled on it cautiously. The room came into light.

In the corner, beside the blue furnace, laying on the cold concrete floor was a bright yellow glue trap, the kind we used to catch furry long legged crickets that often infested the basement. Laying inside it was a small dark brown mouse. He was cute. He was struggling. He fought the glue that trapped him and squeaked in terror.

I panicked. What should I do? I certainly couldn't peel him off the glue trap that would be impossible. Did I have the guts to put him out of his misery and 'dispatch' him with a final blow? No. I did not have that level of gumption yet. Definitely not. So sheepishly I turned away, pulled the string cutting out the light, and closed the door behind me.

All night I laid there. The clock had since struck midnight moving us into early morning hours of the 22nd. We'd cleared the day of prophecy. Through the night I listened to the mouse struggle. And I found a strange peace there. There was no avoiding it. There was only acceptance. I knew that my entire world had indeed ended. Dad would be dead soon and my whole world had been turned upside down. So an end of days? In a way, yes. Though poetically so. I wasn't afraid anymore to meet the occasion. And that was the moment I took on death as my mistress, my muse, my teacher.

Today is a Good Day to Die

This is a phrase often attributed (and mis-attributed) to Native American culture, whose specific origins are unknown to me, though the message rings crystal clear. The idea being that on all days we must be prepared and at peace to meet our end. That all days in their simplicity, in their steadfast commitment to the daily discipline of sunrise, sunset, tide in, tide out, hold it all. The magic is in the possibility that each day holds, that of expansion. Of joy. Of connection with others and self. Forever in each day is that possibility of the opposite. Of the end. Of the meeting of our maker. The final moment of inhale and last exhale. There is never a bad day to die. Each day is an opportunity to meet life in the way it presents itself to us. Nakedly, and in Love.

My belief is that each of us has a soul path. A sort of agreement we take before coming into this incarnation. You can think of it as a set of lessons we choose to come down and learn, a group of people we predetermine to meet, fall in love with, betray, kill, birth, and the list goes on. It is a cycle of what some call karma. Where in each life we accumulate karma and in each life we burn off a bit. So in that sense my belief, though sometimes hard to swallow, is that we each have a predetermined set of experiences to go through and gifts to share. When that life path is done, it is our time to go. You might ask about those who are gone too soon. Certainly, this is very sad indeed because we often think of the long lives they could have lived. Though I find a strange solace in this idea that when a person's time is done, they're ready to be on their way.

I think of it for myself and know that if I were to die today, it would mean I had shared and given all I needed to in this life. I had loved those I needed to, I had fulfilled the soul contracts of hurting certain people, disappointing others, uplifting some, inspiring others, learning certain things, teaching others. I had done all I was meant to. So in this way I cannot be sad that someone dies. To me it means they fulfilled their soul mission. Short or long though it may have been. The lessons that those left behind learn from that departure are magnificent and far reaching. How else could we learn how to love more deeply through our grief? How else would we have learned radical forgiveness? Or how to come into compassion for self and others through this?

We learn by completing these cycles of karma and contracts with others. Like one big school of life! We are souls having a human experience. So yes! It is a fun one in many ways and so very hard in others. Doesn't mean we give up and live in a nihilistic way (though go for it if that is your aesthetic!). Instead we can choose to embrace life more fully. Come into deeper appreciation for the subtleties and exquisite detail we can find in each passing moment. In each gust of wind that comes, in each leaf of a flower, in the tears that stream down our faces one by one. Each one a tiny miracle here to add to the sensory experience of life on earth. Sad to leave, of course, that can be there too, but happy to have lived to begin with.

Death as a spiritual practice can take many forms and I encourage you to seek out what floats your boat. There are many avenues to come into greater contact with the vastness that death presents us with.

Here are a few to think about:

- **Sensory deprivation - float tanks**
- **Yoga Nidra**
- **Burial ritual: be ritualistically buried in soil or sand *ask around your community and find a reputable practitioner you trust***
- **Single pointed focus meditations**
- **Shamanic journeying to meet the moment of your death**
- **Facilitating an ego death *under careful guidance & supervision***

EMOTIONAL RELEASE TOOLKIT:

Letting Go, Letting In

NAME OF THE TOOL
Emotional Release Toolkit
Letting Go, Letting In

BRIEF DESCRIPTION

Transmute stuck energy and take a power stance.

SET THE CONTAINER

Set aside a 5-10 minute container. Light a candle, incense, cast a circle (of white light), whatever floats your boat. Bring into this space a bowl of water to represent the landscape of your emotions and the element of water. Bring a representative of fire: a candle, a match, earth: some actual dirt, a stone. You are the ether / spirit / soul.

PRAYER /AFFIRMATION

I acknowledge the emotions that I've been holding on to. As I let go, I allow Mother Earth to hold me. I am cleansed by earth, air, fire, and water. I am Spirit. By acknowledging my emotions I set them free.

Defrag Your Aura

One of my ultimate all time fave ways to get back into my body is to do a basic energetic sweep of the bod. Super simple to do and it can be done anytime, anywhere. For as short or as long a time you need. All you need are your two hands, your breath and awareness. All you have is your breath and awareness? Can't waive your arms around where you're at right now because you have to pretend to be a normal human? Maybe you have no arms. All good. Just use your imagination and allow the mirror neurons to do their thang. Read along and practice.

Focus on your heart, come into awareness of your breath
Kiss your palms together in front of your chest
Notice the place where your feet or seat meets the floor
Lift your crown skyward, dip your chin slightly down
Notice the subtle energy shift within the body
Begin breathing deeply — close your eyes at any time if it feels okay to do so
Slowly begin lifting your palms up the central channel skyward

**Allow the palms to part and split open as your
arms open wide**
**Sweep the space around you from top to bottom using
wide open strokes**
Like the canopy of a palm tree
**Practice inhaling as your bring the palms together and
lift skyward**
Exhale as the palms descend toward the floor
Begin again — repeat as needed
Inhaling up, Exhaling Down

As you practice you'll begin to notice subtle differences in certain places within your energetic sphere. You may notice certain parts feel tender to pass through, sensing a bit of resistance perhaps. This is totally normal and okay! Continue practicing and bring a sense of love into the action as you sweep through and clear whatever blockages present themselves. You'll notice after 3-5 breaths a palpable shift within yourself.

Come back to this anytime you need. Wonderful to do at the beginning, middle, and end of the day to check in and sweep out any negativity or big feels that come up. Let it all go. Remember: you are your own guru so practice and see what feels best and how you can use the Aura Defrag in your daily life. Pro-tip: transmute any doo-doo vibes by flicking the energy off your fingertips into the earth, the flame of a candle, the sun, a bowl of water filled with Himalayan salt & soil, or imagine a violet flame in front of you and blast that sh*t away right into the fire. Shazam!

An Ancient Practice: The Eyeball Exercise

This one is a little freaky-leeky so best to practice alone. You'll soon see why you might not want to sit on the subway doing this one. But hey, we're all bozos on this bus, so if you want to, go for it!

The Basics of the Eyeball Exercise

This is a rather ancient yogic technique that is incredibly useful in this day and age. Many of us spend countless hours in front of computer and phone screens which leaves our eyes totally tapped out. When was the last time you gave your eyes a little love? Eating a ton of carrots doesn't count, y'all. Listen up.

Find a comfortable seat and begin by placing your first & middle finger at the center of your forehead (thumb and pinky rest gently either side of the nose).

Look up towards 12 o'clock - inhale & exhale:
> **Work your way clockwise taking deep breaths as you stretch the eyes toward the far reaches of each corner of your periphery.**
>> **You may notice a bit of tenderness as you do this, it is normal! You may be using muscles you haven't accessed in a while.**

Once you've finished a full rotation, begin again going counter clockwise:
> **As you go, notice there may be certain areas which are difficult either physically or emotionally painful to look at. Just notice.**

Begin playing with shifting directions.
> **Look from 12:00 to 6:00, 3:00 to 9:00 and so on.**

Get into the diagonals even! 1:00 to 7:00, 11:00 to 5:00. Get loco with it.
Breathe as you go, googly eyes.

You may choose to keep this as your practice or bring in the use of affirmations. Often the parts of our vision that are too painful to 'look' at the mirror are indeed facets of our lives that we can't bear facing. Feel into what you're needing when these feelings come up. Is it a lack of self love, self forgiveness, regretting the past, fear of the future?

Tailor your affirmations to your wanted outcome.

Affirmations to try:

- **I love myself**
- **I forgive myself**
- **I am safe in my body**
- **The future is bright for me**
- **I release and forgive the past**

Breathe deeply as you work your way around the clock repeating the affirmation each time you reach the next hour on the clock.

If there is a certain area that is particularly painful you may choose to spend more time there and breathe into that space, allowing it to stretch and release.

Aftercare:

- **Rub your palms together vigorously**
- **Firmly press your palms into your eyes**

- Press your thumb knuckles in to the space between your eyes and your brow bone
- Trace a semi circle down towards your temples: press small circles there
- Press your thumb knuckles across the top brow bone
- Trace a semi circle down toward your temples: more small circles
- Allow the eyes to rest and close
- Sit in quiet contemplation for a few minutes and allow for integration

EFT

This stands for "Emotional Freedom Technique" and was introduced to me by a kooky friend who did nude modeling for art classes and needed a tool to calm her nerves before de-robing in front of 25 strangers. There are plenty of how-to tutorials you can find online, though I like my version best which is simple self discovery! EFT helps to calm the nervous system with repetitive gentle tapping of certain meridians, energy points and centers. You can play around and see what you feel at each point and which are most useful to you in different situations.

The technique:

- Take the first two fingers and curl the ring & pinky finger into your palm til you look like a medieval saint in an old oil painting.
- Gently tap your fingers repeatedly on each point, lingering in each spot for a minute or two as needed.

Points to tap:

- **Middle of the chest, the sternum**
- **The space between the eyebrows**
- **The space beneath the nose above the lips**
- **The chin**
- **Above the outer edge of each eyebrow**
- **The outer edge of the pinky side of the palm (alternate hands)**
- **The base of the skull**

Play around and tune into how you feel at each point.

This tool is great to use when emotions are bubbling up, before or during a tough conversation, calming the nerves while using public transportation or being in crowds. The uses are endless.

Power Stances

One of my fave tricks to instantly feel more grounded, empowered and in my body is to take a power stance. Long used by overcompensating CEO's, sheriffs, and superheroes, the power stance is ripe for the grief walker to take on as their own. Try these out and see how you feel.

The Stances:

- **Hands on the hips, feet wider than hips distance apart, chest up, belly soft & protruding.**
  - ◇ **Option to perch a foot on a ledge or stool, open up the hips. *Great to use in scary social situations, when you want to feel in control and at ease.***

- **Arms raised in a wide V, palms outstretched, big smile.**
  - ◇ **Perfect for holding while breathing triumphantly on a summit, or casually in your kitchen while brewing your morning coffee. Charge yourself up for the day!**

- **Goddess pose: feet wide, toes turned out, knees bent 90° angle, palms on knees are outstretched with claw-like fingers = ROAR!**
  - ◇ **Works wonders on releasing anger, warding off fears, and harnessing your fierceness.**

- **Stand feet together, palms at heart center.**
  - ◇ **Astounding tool for coming back to your wholeness. Become the central channel of light that you are. Close your eyes, come back to the present moment.**

Slap the Bod

Here I'm taking the age-old practice of "slap the bag" and adapting it to clearing out grief and anger from the body. Because at the end of the day, aren't we all just a nearly emptied bag of boxed wine? Just me? Regardless, hear me out.

This is truthfully taken from different lineages I've learned from, though was first introduced to me by a stern Russian woman while alone with her inside a steam room at the public pools on Long Island. As the sound of the hissing steam pipes slowly faded away after pouring thick clouds of purifying steam into the white tiled echo chamber of a room, a new sound emerged. I narrowed my eyes to peer through the mist to see the woman sitting naked on the bench slapping the absolute sh*t out of her body. From head to toe she was just *going* for it. And I thought: "wow, I'm kind of intimidated and strangely turned on right now ... she must be on to something."

Indeed she was my friend, for the next time I found myself truly alone in that steam room I went to work. With a cupped open palm I slapped myself from the top of my head, down over my arms, my breasts, my belly, my thighs, all the way down to the soles of my feet. And holy jeebus I must tell you I had never felt so invigorated and alive. The good part is that this can be practiced both in and out of a steam room (large Russian practice partner optional).

Try it out for yourself, the instructions are simple and the benefits are vast. Might feel funny at first but trust me, every cell in your body will come alive. Wonderful for detoxification, clearing stagnant energy, getting the body up and moving especially after long periods of being sedentary.

Extra points if you try out my **Giant's Practice** which looks something like:

- **Curl your fingers into FISTS and begin beating your chest rapidly**
- **Walk your feet out WIDE: take up space**
- **Using your full, BOOMING voice beating your chest as you announce:**
- **"Fee! Fie! Foe! Fum! I smell the BLOOD OF AN ENGLISHMAN!" Repeat and/or add your own affirmations. Stomp your feet. ROAR. GROWL. Behave like the Feral Queen you Are.**

The Giant's Practice is particularly potent and should be performed with utmost caution. Side effects include: feeling like a bad ass Warrior Queen, wanting to pillage local villages, and having an appetite solely for large turkey legs. Get it flowing and start slapping!

FRIENDS:

Reach out. Connect. Receive. Support.

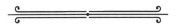

NAME OF THE TOOL
Friends Guide
Reach out. Connect. Receive. Support.

BRIEF DESCRIPTION

Connect to your friends. Ask them and receive their support.

SET THE CONTAINER

Reach out to 2-3 of your besties. Your go-to wild loves. You can request a regular check in if you're going through it and can't do the outreach.

PRAYER /AFFIRMATION

I allow myself to receive the support and help of friends. I lovingly send out the call to the friends who are able to hold space for me.

Friends, gather round: this one goes out to you. Here you are. You made it. You are the lucky person who gets to hold space for your dear friend who is grieving. Cool on you! (Grievers, if you're reading this, it may be helpful to keep in mind).

Here's the thing, we started out friends, it was cool then it was all pretend, hey hey, since you've been gone. We all know the song. The shitty reality of having lost someone is that many friends run for the gosh darn hills. It absolutely sucks. The people who you once thought would always be there, the "ride or die" peeps, suddenly are nowhere to be found. The ultimate ghost. Super shitty. It is wild that this happens though it is completely understandable. Death, illness, and dying is not pretty! Yes, it is literally messy (quite literally in the sh*t, p*ss, blood, and vomit). It is emotionally messy too. It stinks.

For young people, it can be particularly difficult because we lack the depth of experience that most older people have. Chances are most older people have already lost someone who meant a lot to them. The shitty part of being young is that not many of your people have gone through this. Which is why it's understandable that most friends run for those hills perhaps never to be seen or heard from again. Maybe at the funeral as they sheepishly express their condolences, traitor! Anyway, I digress.

The point is, if you're reading this book you are one in a million. You, my friend, are a goddamn gem. Here is the kicker, if you were a ride or die before all this went down, you are now cordially invited to be a life long ride or die from now on until forever and ever. This is serious stuff okay?

You are here because you have been chosen. You have been chosen to take upon yourself a very valiant deed — you are here to support your grieving friend. They will come to you at all hours of the night, morning, and mid-afternoon. You are now this person. You can create boundaries — as they are very important in navigating this emotionally of course. You should value your own time and space while finding the right ways to kindly let your grieving friend know when: "Now is not the time, dear!" Again, speaking this lovingly is the key here.

So you have this task ahead of you. It may be long and trust me when I say there is no end in sight. You are strong though. Perhaps you realized something within yourself that armed you for this journey. You have tools you think may come in handy. Patience? Great. This will help you. Do you have the ability to create a burrito out of a human (not for cannibals of course, but for coziness factors ONLY)? How good are your tent fort building skills? Do you know any traveling masseuses, cake makers, dog walkers, slow talkers, or side-walk chalkers? Bring out all your best tools and your cast of characters. You will need them. Your friend needs you to be just that, a friend. You will become a safe haven for them.

The ultimate key here is instead of offering advice, or solutions, first offer your ear. Offer your time to listen. Offer the ultimate gift of holding space. It can be terrifying at times. Though I must stress to you more over anything else is the importance of holding space. That when one is grieving, it is very scary for your friend, because it can feel as if the entire world doesn't make sense. Like they might spontaneously combust at any moment. Frankly, grieving alone can be quite terrifying, because it feels like the walls and space might crumble around you if you allow yourself to truly wail, cry, let it all out.

Many times I believe people get really uncomfortable with the unabashed releasing of emotions. Like ... what could happen? Really when you think about it? Is us giving them permission to really let go of a secret and silent permission to allow ourselves to do just that? I think so. When we learn how to hold space for our grieving friend, it is a tool that we can call upon for ourselves in the future. You are teaching the future-you how to grieve. How to ask for help. How to hold space for your loved ones. In this way, you learn from your grieving friend. They stand in a portal of neither here, nor there, connected deeply with the spirit world. They remain in a sort of no-place, every-place. They are simultaneously barren, and bursting with fullness. You have a gift sitting in front of you. Learn this mystery. There is so much there to see, if you only give yourself the gift of being-with.

So no matter how loud, or messy, or pathetic, the griever may become, hold it all. You are a spacious container for human experience, lucky you! Come armed with snacks, water, good movies to watch over popcorn, mud masks, nail polish, whatever your griever loves: bring that!

Consider these words by Tara Brach:

> In the Lakota/Sioux tradition, a person who is grieving is considered most wakan, most holy. There's a sense that when someone is struck by the sudden lightening of loss, he or she stands on the threshold of the spirit world. The prayers of those who grieve are considered especially strong, and it is proper to ask them for their help.

You might recall what it's like to be with someone who has grieved deeply. The person has no layer of protection, nothing left to defend. The mystery is looking out through that person's eyes. For the time being, he or she has accepted the reality of loss and has stopped clinging to the past or grasping at the future. In the groundless openness of sorrow, there is a wholeness of presence and a deep natural wisdom.

—Tara Brach, *True Refuge: Finding Peace and Freedom in Your Own Awakened Heart*

Want to hear a little sob story? When I was going through this I had like *no* friends. And I don't say that to sound harsh. Or to beg for your sympathy. The truth is, when this all happened many friends ran for the freaking hills. The friends that I felt would be there through thick and thin who were absolute ride or dies just simply, did not show up. I found myself totally alone. Confused. Scared. And I needed a friend more than anything.

I had people who would come and show their basic levels of kindness. But when it got too intense and emotional they jumped ship. We were young and I can't really blame them. I know they felt totally inept and without a handbook. They were too afraid to say the wrong thing, or not be able to hold the pain. It was hard for them to witness the scary world of death and dying. When their lives were youthful, and filled with hope, diving into my world seemed scary, I'm sure. Still, I gave many of them opportunities to show up.

I asked an old boyfriend to come play music for my Dad as he was dying. The one thing he kept asking for over and over was for my ex boyfriend to come and play for him. I called him up, and he couldn't find the right words to say no. He struggled to tell me that no, it was too hard. He was too out of his depth. Other friends I would call and ask to just come and sit with me. What I wanted and craved most was a witness. I needed to just be seen in my sorrow. I needed to be held and consoled. And it was heartbreaking. I could not understand why so many people who I thought so highly of and felt could handle anything just simply could not. Many of them showed up to the funeral. I wondered why. It felt performative. This was not when I needed them.

I have eventually come into forgiveness for this all. I know people have their limits. Did it break my heart? Absolutely. Though I was able to find compassion for the unforgivable. They had their limits. What I found even more curious was that the people who I did not anticipate showing up, actually did. Perhaps an unwelcome stranger into my strange world. I felt sort of bemused. Like, really? You want to be here? They were not my closest of friends. And when I think of it really there was only one. She would show up unannounced with all sorts of things to help. Still with her help I felt alone and I knew it was a lot for her to handle. And she was only one person. At times when I really wanted to dissolve into a puddle of tears in someone's arms, my poor one friend could not bear to hold that. So I cried in my own arms on the floor.

Where were my oodles of friends I'd accumulated through my travels? Still the people came in the way that they could. And I wished they had some sort of tool box to draw from. To show that they were equipped to see this all. To hold it. And to maintain their centers as they did. What to do with friends that actually want to help, but feel completely and totally inept? When you are confronted with death at an age where most people may have only buried a dog, the truth is not a lot of people around you will have the skills to support you.

So here's what to do when being there feels awkward. Awful. When you're scared of doing it wrong, saying the wrong thing, overstepping, causing discomfort. People feel so alone in this experience. Death is one of life's big teachings. So this is what I would have liked to receive:

- **Presence. Pure and simple.**
- **Listening.**
- **Witnessing.**

There's safety and medicine we can create for each other during these experiences.

Supporting Your Friend: Do This, Not That

DO THIS
- Empathic listening
- Holding space
- Showing up
- Gently offer options (go for a walk, watch a movie, do a yoga class)
- Ask before offering physical touch

NOT THAT
- Gaslight their feelings: "oh come on it isn't *that* bad"
- Give them false hope: "I'm sure they'll get better!"
- Make statements about their loved one's death: "At least they went quick"
- Put them on a grieving timeline: "it's been 6 months, get over it already!"

GRIEFCATION®:

It's time to take a break, beloved.

NAME OF THE TOOL
Griefcation®
It's time to take a break, beloved.

BRIEF DESCRIPTION

Your Griefcation® awaits: book time away, a big trip or a staycation.

SET THE CONTAINER

Tell your work you need time off. Tell your friends you need them to (water your plants, take care of your kids, watch your dog.) You may get some No's. You will get Yes's. And you'll be ready to pack up and go. Your destination is UP TO YOU: it could be a weekend staycation, a local getaway, or on the other side of the bloody world. It's up to you. It's YOUR Griefcation® after all.

PRAYER /AFFIRMATION

When I say yes to giving to myself what I know I need, I allow myself to fully receive the medicine of Grief's holy experience.

Congratulations, You've Won a Dream Vacation!

Bulbs flash around a bright neon sign as a game show host with a blindingly white smile in a crisp blue suit shakes my hand while he hands me a plane ticket with my name written in bold.

"You're on your way to Cancun, Mexico, where the sun is as bright as the drinks are strong!" I am whisked off in a shiny black limousine to the private jet. Awaiting me are the white sand beaches, the margaritas, and warm, clear blue waters teeming with colorful fish. This is it. The dream vacation I've needed for months ... if not years.

I used to play this scenario around in my head while I grappled with the grief of Dad's cancer. I wanted it all to be over. Or that it was all some sort of big, cosmic joke. I waited for this game show host to ambush me on the street, on the train, in my car, and congratulate me. Telling me I had done it, I had won! Not only was my Dad miraculously now in perfect health, but we would all be flown to a dream destination vacation. This didn't happen in the exact way I had imagined. There was no game show host. Though I highly recommend going on a sad walk to "Talk Show Host" by

Radiohead if you're in that neighborhood. Doesn't quite have the same effect but you get my drift.

"I want to be someone else or I'll explode"
Radiohead, Talk Show Host

I wanted to float upon the surface for the birds. You dig?

So.

YOU. DESERVE. A. VACATION.

You heard that right. It is time to take a trip. Sure! They say that you don't have to go to the Himalayas to reach enlightenment, but a change of scenery sure does help! My suggestion to you is, if it is at all possible, book yourself a Griefcation®. We all need some time off when dealing with grief. This could be during your anticipatory grief period or after the passing of your loved one.

My trip after my Dad passed was to Australia then Bali. I wanted to get as far away as possible from the people who knew me, who knew him, and everything familiar. I'd never been to that side of the world and I figured that was far enough away from the groups of people whose heads seemed to snap in half to the side each time they'd see me.

With this sad look on their faces they'd express their condolences, or hug me, even worse! It wasn't what I wanted or needed. I wanted to be as far away from who I had been in that time of illness and death. I wanted to be somewhere no one knew me and all around me was different. Where I could navigate a completely different culture and process my own grief as I did. Along the way I would meet fantastic friends I hold to this day.

I chose to first land in the arms of a couple I'd met during my Peru adventure. They would be holding a healing retreat in the Byron Bay hinterland (sort of like a boho-hippie-chic mecca). It was heaven. I was able to completely unravel within this group, and from there I felt I had the strength to carry on my adventure in a space of eager anticipation and open heartedness. All I had to do was get on the plane and go. A month after my Dad's passing I was flying 15 hours to the other side of the world. Warm beaches, hot Aussie accents, and wonderful food, culture, and fashion. That led me to having a healing love affair with a local "Straya" man, which then led to my next destination of Bali to continue my journey.

This is all to say that you have my full permission to take a trip. Listen, I know it isn't accessible to all or even feasible. I know we all lead lives and there may be kids, family members, and people who depend on you. Is it possible though that you may be able to step away for a week or two? Perhaps a month? Would your support network be able to give you that space? Ask your group and you can find this. I know it. Even if it is a weekend away at a local Airbnb.

Take the time to take yourself out of the ordinary circumstances of your life. What would you most like to experience? What have you missed most lately? If possible find a place close to nature (as in my belief, nature is our greatest teacher and healer). Take the space to reach the inner depths of your soul and nourish it deeply. Good food, a nice swim, perhaps a massage, and an exotic lover. This is your time now. If you feel resistance to this check in with yourself: death is a great reminder and mirror on how we are with ourselves, our own process, how much we can step into new spaces with ourselves. New depths too.

I was fortunate to work with multiple gifted shamans, healers, massage therapists, and yoga teachers during my healing trip. This time was invaluable. Yes, it was lonely at times, being so far away from everyone I knew. Thankfully the technology we have today is a great gift in that I could video chat with my friends and family whenever I needed to. The other plus of traveling alone is that I met so many fantastic people along the way. Open to anything, the world presented me with a fantastic cast of characters who nurtured and informed my journey. I received the gifts of wisdom from people I met randomly seated next to in a restaurant, in lotus alongside my yoga mat, randomly passing by a cafe as I sat outside reading *The Power of Now*. Each moment has a gift. A wisdom. And to give ourselves that space to discover that is immense.

Nowadays in modern mourning we are taught to just "get over it." "You're still grieving??" people may ask insensitively. Yes, of course you are and you can take all the time you need. My wish is that more of us can give ourselves permission to take that time out. No rush to get back to work in a daze two weeks later. Crowdfund your Griefcation® if you need to. See chapter on "let me know if you need anything". Now is the time for your crew to show up and help you out. Take a trip, you may be astounded by who and what you may find. Yourself? Again, after the loss? My guess is: most likely. Dive in and get out there.

THE HERO'S JOURNEY:

Separation. Initiation. Return.

NAME OF THE TOOL
The Hero's Journey
Separation. Initiation. Return.

BRIEF DESCRIPTION

Discover your inner hero / heroine

SET THE CONTAINER

Set aside 20-25 minutes for a journaling practice.

Journal prompts:

- When was the call to adventure? What was the challenge ahead of me?
- Did I resist the call at first? Why? What was I afraid of?
- What tools or magical items did I receive? Think family heirlooms, crystals, power stones, photographs, etc. How did it bring me luck/hope/perseverance?

- Who Mentored me during my Hero's Journey? What wisdom did they share? In what moments did I go to them for advice?
- What did I encounter in the underworld? What battles did I fight? What fears did I conquer? Who/what were my foes?
- Returning to society or the normal world, what are my gifts? What wisdom do I have to share and how can I serve it to my community?

PRAYER /AFFIRMATION

I am willing to see myself as the Hero / Heroine of this story. I know that there's a bigger plan for me. I am not a victim. I am the hero(ine). And I always have been.

Sitting at a small circular table in an outdoor cafe on a quiet roadside in Bali, I stared at a book gifted to me by the girl named Blu called "The Power of Now". Distracted by an overly loud conversation between a father and daughter at a nearby table, my eyes narrowed and my brow furrowed as I attempted to focus on the words across the page of the aqua blue book. I resented the father/daughter duo while simultaneously envying them. Damn them and their loud conversation about what smoothie bowl they would order! Next to them sat a young tourist couple. Newlyweds? They were arranging their plates finding the best angle to snap photos for their Instagram feed no doubt. Eye roll. How pedestrian.

Out of the corner of my eye, a flurry of energy bounding down the spiral staircase from the cafe's balcony above came a bright female American voice.

"That's a great book!" the voice exclaimed with all the joie de vivre of a puppy happily meeting a stranger on the street. How could she be so optimistic and happy? Who was this person? I was intrigued while the pessimist I'd embodied a moment ago wanted to be put off.

I shifted my demeanor. This was an opportunity.

"I know right?" I beamed back. Standing in front of me was a Midwestern American girl named Joni. Affixed to her nose was a golden hoop. She wore the usual Bali attire of tightly fitted yoga clothes. Her smile seemed to say "I'm friendly". And her eyes communicated that tad bit of crazy wisdom that I knew would be my cup of tea. I learned she was a former peace corps volunteer who was currently teaching English to students on Lombok, a neighboring island. She had the grit of someone who'd seen the hardships that traveling exposes you to, and the kindness of someone who'd seen the goodness in all people here to teach us.

She held the wisdom of the women she'd worked with in remote areas of Morocco. Building centers for women to learn about family planning, contraception, abortion. It was tough work and the language barrier had taught her how to communicate in the words between words. How to say certain things with your eyes and hands. She had a way with language. Speaking Indonesian nearly fluently with her Ohio American accent. Ohio for god's sake! How did she get so far from home?

Within an hour of meeting we were rhythmically flailing together as new friends at the local ecstatic dance in the open air "Yoga Barn". Later on we sat outside that same cafe on the second floor balcony overlooking the rooftops of Ubud, with their auburn colored tiled roofs. Palm trees poking out between buildings. The omnipresent scent of incense wafting through the air.

She pulled out her tarot card deck and did a spread to help determine where I was at in my grieving process. At the top was a card called "The Tower". A person tragically falling from the top of a castle. I saw this as me. My castle was toppling though I felt optimistic. Beneath it sat "The High Priestess' '. I felt instinctively this was a potent spiritual learning even though painful, yes. Knowing through this I would come to embody that energy of a powerful magician woman. And of course my friend "The Fool" came to visit in this spread. Always reminding me to keep a sense of humor as I journeyed into the unknown. Optimistic and carrying all necessities on my back.

There was a sort of mythology building here. I could see it through the spread of colorful cards Joni had laid out in front of us between our matcha green lattes.

"Have you ever heard of Joseph Campbell?" Joni asked. I shook my head, no. She leaned in: "Oh you're in for a treat!" she whispered as she excitedly pulled a book from her travel worn knapsack. In her hands was a thick book called "The Hero with A Thousand Faces" by fellow New York native, Joseph Campbell.

She told me: "You're on a journey now, and you're the hero of this story. Read this book and you'll see how you're just like every hero of every myth, legend, movie, and story ever written. He lays it all out here."

Dumbfounded, I took the book from her hands. What began as a simple conversation soon took me on a month-long journey of silent retreat as I cleansed my body and dove into Campbell's work.

An ayurvedic panchakarma involves 21 days of a strict elimination diet, designed to pacify any imbalances within the doshas. A dosha is sort of like a personal constitution. How we are naturally built can get out of whack when we overindulge or behave in certain ways, like when we let our emotions get the best of us. Grief can totally get the system out of whack and boy was my body in need of some fine tuning and re-calibration. Every morning begins with a tablespoon of clarified butter, or Ghee, infused with ayurvedic medicinal herbs. Then begins a daily ritual of steam baths, sesame oil massages, herbal concoctions, yoga, and meditation. At a certain point you go through huge purgation where you're given a vile tasting drink that brings about a violent, daylong, diarrhea extravaganza. The doctor stopped counting after my 70th trip to the loo. Luckily I had my boy Joseph to provide context through all of this.

It was the perfect opportunity to do a deep dive into my own healing, and get to the bottom of what this whole Hero's Journey was about. Every day in between treatments I would lay on the cool cream tiled floors of my villa and listen to the audio book as I rolled out my violently detoxing body with massage balls. As I unlocked deep-set beliefs, memories, and traumas within my body, I learned how my travails were not altogether dissimilar from our best-loved heroes and heroines. Suddenly I was Kali Ma, the fierce goddess with her tongue unswirled stomping on the body of Shiva wearing a mala of dripping bloody heads, fierce, fearless.

Creation and destruction all in one. As I birthed myself into this world of mythology I saw how I was the divine mother, the sacred prostitute, the wounded healer, the prophet, the oracle, the betrayer, the savior. I could see myself within all the parables that Campbell compared. Through his regaling of the great love stories and adventures of the most celebrated heroes and the most reviled villains, I began to see the similarities. They were all the same. Duh! Campbell's work goes to show us that somehow miraculously within all world cultures and stories that have been passed down over lineages these stories had a through line that united us all. Between grandmothers and grandsons, rites of initiation of young women and men, the birth of our youth and the dying of our elders. They all followed what Campbell calls: "The Hero's Journey".

Now, you most definitely will want to check out his work so please, allow me to give my meager attempt at describing this journey, while keeping in mind the man dedicated his entire life to this. Okay? The Hero's Journey follows a basic wheel of events that are usually described with a handy diagram.

There is the call to adventure, when the hero first learns of the opportunity to go off and seek/avenge/rescue/destroy/whatever the call is. Luke Skywalker gets the message while refurbishing R2D2 from the ethereal Princess Leia that he must save her and her planet Alderon. Often there is the refusal where the hero is overwhelmed or is like "Heck no that sounds wild, I'm not about to risk life and limb to go do x_____ .

Usually they are gifted some sort of tool or talisman to guide them. Some magical thing that will aid them, give them special powers to navigate the new and uncharted territory.

They are met with a mentor who will guide their way. Think Gandalf (one of my personal faves), Obi Wan Kenobi, The Genie in Aladdin, Yoda (duh!). This person will teach them the special skills they'll need to defeat X, conquer X, save X ... you get the drift!

They begin their descent into the underworld where they undergo the initiation (more on this in the next chapter!) this is where they'll meet their foes, battle the overlords, walk through the darkness, go through their self doubt, things fall apart and they figure out how to fix it and keep going!

Once they've rescued the girl, saved the kingdom, destroyed the ring, etc — then begins their return to society where they learn how to share the gifts and lessons they learned. Pretty cool, huh? Yeah! So this is where I started thinking "hey this sounds a lot like what I just went through". And dang that helped a lot! I began to connect the dots. I began to think of the journey through my Dad's illness and death as my own Hero's Journey. I saw all the ways in which I had been the hero of the tale and had gone through my own initiation through trials and tribulations.

So here is where you come in, dear reader. I invite you to connect with your own Hero's Journey. Think through your experience and write yourself into your own parable. So get out a piece of paper or your journal and play around. See the tool at the start of this chapter and have at it, creators.

Remember this is your story and you can color it in any way you choose. It also helps to keep in mind that it might not exactly fit in this tidy recipe because life often gives us multiple hero's journeys all rolled into one. So pick and choose how you write yours and know that it is all completely valid. For me, it was helpful to know it can be a freaking trilogy! Like every chapter of my Dad's illness was a different call to adventure. The diagnosis, the surgery, the journey into a world of death, the spiritual gifts of intuition and ESP I received, the elders who guided me, the self discovery trips I went on, returning with the gifts to share with my Dad during his illness — only to begin it all again as the next treatment began, the next prognosis was delivered, the next round of doctors came around. You get the drift. This is your story, and your life, your own movie to direct and star in.

I'll leave you with this one little story from my Griefcation® in Bali. During the June full moon I traveled far out into the rice fields on my bright red moped guided only by a floating dot on my apple maps and the light of the moon illuminating the small dirt path in front of me. Driving in the direction of an under the radar traditional Balinese healer named Agus.

We began a three night long Full Moon ceremony unlike any I had ever experienced before. Each night I would dress in ceremonial Balinese garb. Bright pink silk clothes, and patterned batik skirts. Each night was a different experience. A whirlwind of flowers, incense, and prayers, and barefoot trips into the rice fields to stand beneath the moon as I was prayed upon and sprayed with holy water.

One night he sat me in a deep, cold bathtub, the room lit by candles. The cool powder blue tiles surrounded me as I lowered myself into the bath. For a seemingly endless amount of time I sat in this cold bath as Agus prayed outside the door behind me. This wasn't just any bath. This was a flower bath. The entire tub was filled with pounds and pounds of brightly colored flower petals. Flower petals were Agus' "thing". I sat and sat as I stewed and marinated. First feeling blissful and "oh wow this is so special" then ... "okay this is getting a bit cold I really want to get out"... until "holy jesus will this ever end I can't believe it has been this long and is this kind Balinese man really still outside praying over me while I sit in here disgruntled and hugging my body to keep warm."

Was I not spiritual enough? Finally he brought me out, wrinkled and shivering, and we began the next rites. The Flowers. Never. Stopped. Each ceremony involved me being covered in handfuls and handfuls of flower petals. Once on a bed, in a small chamber surrounded in gold. Once in a room in complete darkness as I was instructed to pray to the directions and ask for forgiveness. By night three as I drove out alone into the rice fields I was beginning to feel something shift. It felt magical, yes, but also a bit grueling. Hard to describe. It felt like a peeling off of layers, one by one. Come out of one pile of flowers, enter another. I mean, really? Yes.

Finally on the end of the third night Agus sat me down on a silk golden cushioned bench and took my hands in his. He stared at the lines across my open faced palms. He told me I was a traveler. Of course. He told me I would always be traveling and learning. Going from place to place. Gypsy like. Okay. Yep, got it. He told me I would always need to live within nature. I could go into cities briefly but I had to come back out and stay within nature. Got it, noted. Then he said something that I somehow always knew and yet after these dizzying days of flower petal ceremony, it suddenly hit home.

He carefully looked at me, narrowing his eyes and said: "This is your life. You're the star of your own movie and you can make, create, and do anything you want. Think of it from outside that perspective. You're the star of your own adventure, make it what you want."

Obviously this was my Neo-meets-the-oracle moment, right? You feel me. This is your Hero's Journey, you're the Hero. The Heroine. Make it freaking fab.

IGNITE THE FLAME:

Entering Into Initiation

NAME OF THE TOOL
Ignite the Flame
Entering Into Initiation

BRIEF DESCRIPTION

Embracing the medicine of a Rite of Passage / Ceremony.

SET THE CONTAINER

Sometimes you have the option in your life to go into initiation. Whether that's through a vision quest, a ceremony. But you can very well do it yourself. Because, after all. You got da power. That may be going to a local place in nature that calls to you and meditating. Dancing. Letting yourself drop into a space. You can literally go into your nearest water (providing it's safe) and be baptized. It's between you and the Creator, anyway.

PRAYER /AFFIRMATION

I acknowledge that a new phase of my life has begun. I am not the same. Like the caterpillar emerging as a butterfly, I claim the full space of my wings.

I'm sitting on a bench in Clinton Hill, Brooklyn one brisk day in Autumn, my birthday in fact, the equinox on September 22nd. My body is still slightly damp from the float tank deprivation chamber I'd just exited. The semi-circle of park benches surrounding a large tree at the center. A playground nearby is full of city kids screaming and playing. Life was life-ing all around me. People surrounded me, yet I was alone. Strangely, somehow content though yearning for more. Connection. Begging for the world around me to somehow acknowledge what had just happened. My mind is calm as if still floating in the warm Epsom salt bath. Drenched in what was now pooling my mind. A new reality. Mom had called just as I'd exited the soft salt womb of the float tank. The results had come in from the doctors. The last hope of clinical trials had failed and Dad's new prognosis was clear. It wouldn't be long now and we had to prepare for what? The worst? Or a new beginning?

I wondered as I sat beneath the shade of the tree. I looked around at the humans passing by, sitting on the benches next to me. My mind was still and yet my heart wanted to leap out of my chest and grab the next person I saw by the shoulders, violently shaking them to say: "Hey! My Dad is about to die!" It felt alien to be sitting next to people minding their days, walking their grocery trolley, blowing bubbles with their children, sitting eating a subway sandwich, living their normal everyday life. While there I was, somehow surrounded in this opaque bubble of unfamiliar strangeness. A soft suspension of the indescribable. I was the same and yet different. It was an initiation. How could I be held then? Where was my tribe? If not here, then where? And how could I create my own way?

We often look for ways to mark the line of change between the what-has-been to the not-yet-to-be. The dyeing of hair after a failed relationship. The new wardrobe before the beginning of a new school year. A shifting of personas. Like putting on a new pair of clothes. We're different and yet it may take some time to settle in. It feels almost alien, breaking in the new self.

Have you been feeling the urge to make some huge radical shift since your life has changed? Wanting to shave your head, go into the woods and live in silence? Craving a rite of passage that marks your new life that has somehow shifted in what may feel like a blink of an eye. Our culture often ignores these rites. In other cultures, there are grand spectacles for each passing of life's experiences. The men's groups go out into the jungle to learn from the elders and go through their own tests to become men and enter back into the tribe. The women marking the passage of a girl into a woman when she gets her first bleed.

There are initiations into secret societies, religious groups, or medicine wisdom keeper circles. Often we are left alone as we know we are somehow very different and yet there aren't any practices set up to acknowledge this. Where have they gone? Silenced by colonizers, shunned, made to be seen as radical or evil. They have been systematically erased until all we have is a small whisper that comes on the wind as a leaf travels down while we sit on a park bench alone in Brooklyn wondering. How? There must be someone, anyone, who should be here telling me that: Yes, this is a big moment for you. Where are they? Where have they gone? Why are we having to navigate this alone?

I took it upon myself to find out. To learn new ways of initiating myself and finding the teachers who would see it and give it merit.

Again I'm in Bali. Receiving a reiki healing from a small waif-like Australian crone named Devi Ma. Her high pitched voice, wide set eyes, and thin crinkly hands wafted over my body looking for imbalances. Balancing them and clearing blockages, some of them ancient ones. With her own songs, her own personal magic. I held back giggles as she moved the work through my body releasing loud belches each time an old blockage was released. My body quaked and my legs shook uncontrollably. I had visions of purple light taking over my body, healing and flooding my limbs. Past life memories of dying from childbirth played behind my eyelids. Covered in blood, feeling the life force drain from my body. The sadness of having to leave behind a loving family. Memories of lives spent in Egypt as a seductress and powerful sex magician. Oh yes, baby.

After an hour or so we were finished and I sat up, somehow totally refreshed and reborn. My spine rising higher, my crown lifting skyward and I felt taller than I'd ever been. Had I grown? Little Devi Ma sat in front of me, her small toned and tanned body draped in a white Balinese draped dress with golden trim. Smiling wide, she looked at me. My chest rose up, and I felt like the Queen of Sheba. She looked at me as if greeting me for the first time. My eyes felt ancient. A wisdom pulsing through my veins as if remembered from eons past. I was strong in my body. Secure in my confidence. Full of power and balanced femininity.

"It's good to see you again, dear sister," she said smilingly. I'd been reborn and re-calibrated with the ancient wisdom of my past selves. "You're undergoing an initiation. The ancient mystery schools are within you and your task now is to learn from their quiet strength and wisdom. The secrets will come through when you become quiet. Simplify your mind. Clear the body. Transmute the old wounds and trauma from your flesh. Learn from the elders and bring this new wisdom onto the earth, dear one. You are greatly needed now." And with that she sat back, closed her eyes and went into a deep silence.

"Wow, okay. Cool." I thought to myself. Yet somehow none of this was casual. I knew in that moment that I had been seen truly for who I have been. For who I am becoming. It was the knowing of initiation into the next self. The wisdom body self.

When life gives us these opportunities for growth here is the real calling: go deeper into the Self and come into gnosis. No biggie. But, yes, you were born for this. You are your own guru and the language of life is here to teach you. What can come is the teaching of your own true mystery school. How do you want to live this? Explore this? What are some rituals or rites of passage you can create or invite into your life experience? Remember this doesn't have to mean going deep into the jungle and learning from a rafiki type character (though it doesn't hurt!). Remember it can be quite simple. Think back to the small rituals you recall from your childhood. Baptisms. Lighting votive candles in cathedrals. Getting your high school diploma.

Receiving. Yes if we think carefully, we can see that the bedrock of what we crave in terms of community and acknowledgment have been there, though quite quiet in their delivery. How can we maximize this for our own journeys? You deserve to know that your process of initiation into becoming a death walker is huge. Don't let the people tell you that grief is as simple as a two week time off of work. This is big work.

So here is the call: create an initiation ceremony for yourself. Know this is the time to move into your power. Time for you to take up space and live from your truth. Your time is now. Go deep, dear one. You are seen.

JOURNALING:

Recording As to Remember

NAME OF THE TOOL
Journaling
Recording As to Remember

BRIEF DESCRIPTION

Record your experience: whether now or later on, you'll be so glad you decided to leave love-notes about who you were and what you were going through.

SET THE CONTAINER

Choose a medium that speaks to you: photography, journaling, collage. Set aside time (anywhere from 10 mins onwards) for you to drop in and create.

PRAYER /AFFIRMATION

Today, I give myself permission to record so that I can remember. I see the beauty in my current experience. Through journaling, I am intimate with myself, I am intimate with my own experience.

When Dad got sick, I started taking photos. More of him than I ever had before. I was documenting his process. The photos I have now are beautiful when I look back on them, however painful they were to take in the moment. Dad sitting at the foggy town dock a few days after his first brain surgery, cowboy hat tipped to the side slightly to cover the blood-caked stitches. A fearful yet serenely penetrating look in his eyes. Or Dad trying to play the guitar again, keeping his fingers busy as his brain attempted to rewire pathways.

So here is the deal, I am gonna invite you to do the same for this process. It will be painful to get your recording device of choice at times, yes. I know it will be. You'll think: "really, right now? I can't possibly record this moment ... it is too grisly, vulnerable, emotional, horrific, ghastly, sad." Whatever. Record it anyway. You will thank me later. You'll thank yourself for sure.

What was also helpful was journaling. Putting pen to paper. Whenever I didn't know what I wanted to say, or felt something that was churning within me and needed an outlet, I could pick up my good ol' moleskine and let it all flow on the pages. Whatever comes out is valid. Even if it is a wild scrawl of anger in large feral letters across the page. That is completely valid. Let it be that. Let it be there. You are right here now experiencing this. The medium is your choice. Find what speaks to you. For some, it may be keeping a voice diary. Recording the voices of their loved ones.

Get down the fantastic story you know they love to tell so that you can have it forever. So you can come back to it when their voice is just a memory. All of those pesky voicemails they'd leave when you had told them never to leave them because you don't check them. You may want to hang on to a few of them. Just to have. Don't hold on too tightly with your fists though. All of life is just a passing through. We cannot keep what we have here. Though we may try to record it.

So pick up your camera, your voice recorder, your paints, your pens, your pencils and just get it down, draw it out. The good, the bad, the ugly, the things that you figure no person would ever want to see the light of day. It is good and it is worthy. Finally I want to share with you my own vision for why I had to pull out my camera and how it helped me. It gave me a filter. It put something between my eyes and what I was seeing before me. Reality was given a barrier. I would put on my fish eye lens and get really close to my father's face as he lay in his hospice bed. He would make funny faces and stare deeply into the lens. That wide-eyed look so singular and distinct to those in their dying space. As if gazing past the veil into the void.

At night when he was struggling with the pain and nausea, I pulled out the camera. Recording the chaotic moments while squirting a shot of morphine into his mouth. Oh that is raw, yes. It is very raw. After he left his body, I pressed the record button to document the serenity of his corpse. How peaceful he looked in the early morning light, surrounded by flowers, candles, and my mother sitting crying quietly. My sister sitting beside her sketching the scene with pencil. And I am glad now I have these memories.

Because while the smiles are lovely to look back on, we must also honor the memories and times when it was hard. Because that part was what made us who we are.

If we cannot record now the life we have lost, we can look back and create something new. Something that honors their existence. Collect old photos of theirs, and make a collage. Get creative. This is your journey. Find what makes your heart sing. Learn to play that piece of music they loved. The parts that are looking to see the light of day. Bring it all out. Put it all down. Record it so that you have it. Claim this time as art.

KICK UP A RUMPUS:

Finding Fun Things to Smash

NAME OF THE TOOL
Kick Up A Rumpus
Finding Fun Things to Smash

BRIEF DESCRIPTION

Release the rage and let yourself go.

SET THE CONTAINER

Find something you can punch. A bed. A couch. A pillow. And go for it. For as long you need to. Ensure that you have a safe space for yourself: meaning you won't be interrupted, and you have support post-rage-a-thon. Like coconut water. Or a blanket.

PRAYER /AFFIRMATION

I express this anger into the fire of divine love. I let the flame purify me. So that I may arise like the Phoenix. Wild and forever free.

> **"Fuck you, I won't do what you tell me/**
> **Fuck you, I won't do what you tell me/**
> **Fuck you, I won't do what you tell me/**
> **Motherf*cker!"**
> "Killing In the Name" — Rage Against the Machine

Lose control. Go ahead. Kick up a gosh darn rumpus, why don't ya? Release the anger. It is okay and safe to do so. This chapter is all about just that. You're angry? Good. Let's transmute that sh*t. One of the things that pissed me off the most was the idea that there was a supposed "process" to grief. Like it was all neat and pretty and if you do it this certain way you're doing it "right." The "5 Stages of Grief", AKA the way it is "supposed" to go according to 2 well known psychologists is:

1. **Denial**
2. **Anger**
3. **Bargaining**
4. **Depression**
5. **Acceptance**

How neat and tidy! That's just great. Not for me, folks! I found I was all over the joint. My grieving was topsy, turvy, every which way ... and I was going through all five stages every day in every which way. It was not cute. Nor is it meant to be, I think.

My opinion is that rage and anger is NORMAL and okay and ... understandable. What is even more important is finding tools to transmute the anger so that we do not accidentally unleash it on an innocent bystander. My view is that everyone is fighting their own battle (yes it may be hokey and belong on a hallmark card but it's true). You may be having the worst possible day: your jacket gets caught on the door handle while rushing out the door, your car won't start, you're outta gas, whatever ... then you're in line trying to get a coffee and the person in front of you is taking forever to decide what kind of macchiato they want (are there more than one kind?) and by then you are a screaming kettle just wanting to burst out and raise hell in this coffee joint. But wait: you remember: *I have tools for this.* Not only can you breathe in that moment, but you remember that yes, I have ways to work through this anger that is bubbling safely, so that I don't worry the entire occupancy of the shop that I'm having a mental breakdown and ordering a 5150 on me. Right? Cool. Here we go.

Here is a comprehensive list of possible ways to release anger:

- **THRASH ABOUT (safely in your own space, careful of your limbs now!)**
- **Kick things (not living)**
- **Go to a shooting range**
- **Punch a bunch of pillows (fuq em!)**
- **Take a hike! Angry stomp your way up the mountain**
- **Pound your fists on your chest as you BELLOW**
- **Stick out your tongue, cross your eyes, and HISS**

- Sing the highest Operatic note you can hit and wait for the glass to shatter
- Dangle your arms while hunched over, uttering low moans as you sway (foam at the mouth for extra points)
- Pat down your body from head to toe: send the energetic residue to the earth, a flame, the sky, or a bowl of warm water and Himalayan salt
- Gather all your unwanted dishes & bowls then *SAFELY* SMASH 'EM! (goggles recommended). Vacuum thoroughly afterward. This is probably not advisable at all but it worked for me IRL
- Scream to the heavens, the void, all four directions
- Go to ecstatic Dance and sweat it out
- Take a sauna then cold plunge: WHOOSH! Arrivederci Anger!
- Massage your liver (take liver supporting herbs — we store anger there)
- Take a five rhythms dance class
- Buy a collection of paints and a large canvas and PAINT IT OUT BB!
- Find a piano and become a bad ass Beethoven (even better if you don't know how to play)
- ETC, ETC, ETC!!!!!

The point here is to *safely* release anger. Let it OUT so that you don't take too much of it IN to your body and soul, dear one. Remember, this is okay and safe to do. It's likely even necessary. If at any point you are fearful of causing harm to yourself or others, it is advisable to seek help. You are not alone! There are trained professionals who can help you work through this.

As with most things in life, I like to create the ultimate soundtrack to cinematize my life — whilst angry jumping on a trampoline, for example.

Here's a list of my fave ANGRY TUNES:

- **"Down with the Sickness" by Disturbed**
- **"Pardon me" by Incubus**
- **"Megalomaniac" by Incubus**
- **"Bulls on Parade" by Rage Against the Machine**
- **"Renegades of Funk" by Rage Against the Machine**
- **"No One Knows" by Queens of the Stone Age**
- **"Feel So Numb" by Rob Zombie**
- **"Hash Pipe" by Weezer**
- **"Blue Orchid" by The White Stripes**
- **"The Hardest Button to Button" by The White Stripes**
- **Pretty much anything by System of a Down**

Honestly I could go on but I actually need to write a book here and not a never-ending playlist.

Good luck! And remember, rage is a normal human emotion! Anger is okay and safe to express in a safe container. You can do all of these exercises alone, or with your trusted friend to watch over you so you don't hurt yourself. Nature is a wonderful friend to witness these practices. She gets it: ever seen a volcano erupt? Exactly, you get the point. Sh*t is WILD and unruly.

Also one final note on the grief stages model. My advice to you is grieve in whatever willy nilly stage you want. My experience has proven that it doesn't follow a tidy track. Instead, it winds and dines and goes every which way like a roller coaster except my phone, keys, eye glasses, and shoes have fallen off. You feel me? This is your journey. And it is okay to be more than a bit pissed off about it.

LET ME KNOW IF YOU NEED ANYTHING:

Ask and Receive

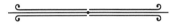

NAME OF THE TOOL
Let Me Know if You Need Anything
Ask and Receive

BRIEF DESCRIPTION

Ask for what you need and be open to receiving it.

SET THE CONTAINER

What is something a friend could do for you that would be helpful? Reach out. Ask for help today. Tune into what you need and reach out for support. If you need to get in touch with what you need, get into a safe somatic space by softly massaging your body, or orienting yourself around a room (simply let your eyes meander and rest on what you enjoy).

PRAYER /AFFIRMATION

I allow myself to receive all that I need. It is strong to ask for what I need and it is healing for me to receive it.

"Let me know if you need anything" they say to you. And it is understandable why they would say such a thing of course. They are wanting to create connection through a way of acknowledging your pain and yet, it leaves us questioning: do they really mean that?

This phrase drove me absolutely nuts for the 3 years Dad was sick. People would slide into my DM's, my texts, my voicemails, my emails to express their condolences and offer their help by saying "let me know if there is anything I can do to help". And it drove me UP THE DAMN WALL. Part of me believed it was a way of absolving themselves of any actual responsibility. Sure, they wanted to let me know they were thinking of me and my loved one but were they actually prepared to do "anything"? And what did "anything" entail? I found myself questioning this over and over again. Mulling it over with every "thanks so much!" text response I sent with a string of emojis to cover my pain. The truth was, I really did need their help. But could I trust them to actually come through when I needed them?

Here's the truth. Most people are not good with death. With not-so-glamorous moments of transition and change and while some ride or die peeps will show up, they may not. You may be terribly disappointed. You may be pleasantly surprised. Allow for both. I say this with a bit of a gritty smile because I learned this the hard way, and you may too. Some friends I thought I could lean on through thick and thin suddenly didn't have a shoulder to lend me when the going got tough. What was even more miraculous was finding out who was still there after the dust settled from the stampede of well wishers bearing lasagnas, flowers, and sappy condolence cards. WHY SO MANY LASAGNAS THOUGH? The hard truth is that some indeed do say these hallmark-ified condolences then aren't actually up to the task. You must choose carefully. Know your audience.

So back to the good news, your ride or dies who show up with their "Let me know if you need anything" messages, take them up on the offer. Call them up and call them out. It's go time. This is where it gets fun. It had me thinking ... they say if I 'need absolutely *anything*' to let them know. So what does that entail? What sorts of things could I ask for help with?

This is where you delegate. What is it that you are *really* needing right now?

For me it was a massage. All the anxious tension I was holding in my body was built up and clenched in my shoulders. This girl needed a good ol' rub down. Plus I was single at the time and one cannot underestimate the healing power of human touch. So the next time a trusted friend asked if there was anything I needed I said: I could really use a massage. A few days later a gift card for the local masseusserie was in my mailbox. I was beyond grateful. That massage cleared away so much of what I had been carrying in my body and the simple act of asking for what I needed broke down all the barriers I had built up around honoring my truth.

Maybe you just need a little help. Feeling super down one day and need someone to pick up the groceries? Ask. Do you want a friend to come over and build a fire with you while you sit in the corner weeping over a glass of wine? Ask. It doesn't matter how strange or seemingly random the ask is. Put yourself into the space of discomfort and ask. I do not say this lightly. I know sometimes the hardest thing to do when grieving is to pick up the phone, respond to a text, or even brush your teeth and get dressed. This is huge and you should be proud of yourself for even asking.

This also applies to any help you need surrounding caring for your loved one or needing support in the aftermath. Maybe your loved one is in hospice and you could use an hour or two to get out for a walk, a manicure, or a cup of coffee. Ask a trusted friend to come by and hold space for your loved one. Maybe you need help piecing through your passed loved one's closet, with each Christmas sweater that passes through your hands like an emotional landmine, knocking you down by it's texture, their smell, the memories of bygone holidays.

When my father passed, we called our neighbor who'd lived down the street from us my entire life. When the undertakers came in their crisp black suits to whisk his earthly shell off on a gurney, it was our neighbor who helped to lift him out of his death bed. We didn't ask her to do this. We had simply asked her to show up. Give people the opportunity to show up and excel in their ability to hold what is present. It is a strange gift to give them. The helping helps them too.

When in grief it can be difficult to discern up from down, let alone knowing exactly what we might need in that moment. So even while we, the bereft may have an inkling of what might help, you, the friend, may offer up some ideas too! Get creative! Get zany!

For our friends of grievers: JUST DO IT. Take initiative and just do what you think might be helpful. Do their grocery shopping. Not sure what they like? Guess. Sending a text to ask might be draining to them and they may feel guilty accepting help. Show up with your dish washing gloves and clean their whole kitchen. Vacuum their rugs. Take their dogs out for a walk. Offer to pick their kids up from school. The point is just keep on showing up with options. You'll never know how much it means to them. They don't always have the energy to tell you exactly what they need. They might not even know! If you can relieve them from that responsibility even for a moment, that would be huge. Don't take it personally if you get it wrong. Just keep doing it.

When Dad went into hospice I moved out of my Brooklyn apartment to be with him. Overwhelmed with the moving process, my roommate said: "let's go buy some groceries, you need to eat too!" When eating was the last thing on my mind, let alone showering (he kindly informed me I needed that too) this lively young man took me to the produce section of our local grocery store and did something that completely shifted the heaviness of my reality. He waltzed with me. Right there amongst the aubergines, crisp romaine heads, and bushels of broccoli: we danced. It was enough to snap me out of my melancholy if only for those few minutes amongst the legumes. Once again I was young and carefree.

Another friend showed up unannounced with a large pot of Indian healing clay and instructed me to get in the bathtub. As I sat there, tears streaming down my face in the warm tub, she slathered a paste of thick olive green clay paste onto my face, neck, and shoulders. Then she sat there on the bathroom floor and held space as I laughed, cried, freaked out at the strange pulsation of my skin responding to the detoxifying clay. Then when it was time to come out and I was fully baked, she laid me down on the white linen bed and sang to me. I was overwhelmed with the release and euphoria the clay had given me. What a gift.

Lastly, I've saved this one because it may be the best, and you know what they say about saving the best for last ...

One brisk New York Autumn day, mid-hospice, a kind acquaintance reached out via social media to ask if I wanted to join a screening Q&A of a new film about an aging Sherlock Holmes played by none other than the myth, the man, the legend: Sir Ian McKellan.

That's right. GANDALF.

Obviously I said yes immediately and planned to take the train into the city later that day, leaving behind the morphine, the urine bottles, and white washcloths at home with Dad. Once again I was free, at least for one evening. Taken out on the town for a moment of fresh air with none other than the White Wizard himself. A man who transcended perceived death and rose once again.

In the dark intimacy of the crowded movie theater, we watched Sir Ian as Mr. Holmes navigate a world of old age and what memories come to be healed as we face our own mortality. The familiar scenes of physical decline returned to fill the silver screen. I was not at home with Dad in hospice, yet I was back there again only now my father was being played by a knight of the realm.

During the Q&A Sir Ian spoke of his experience caring for his own mother as she passed and how that had informed his portrayal. He spoke of the ephemeral importance of that time and how it must be cherished and honored. How our elders have so much to teach us.

Afterwards he held a small reception in the lobby where movie goers could greet him, take a selfie or ask for an autograph. I am never one for these strange shows of idolatry, I tend to respect the person's time and personal space and admire from afar (maybe this is creepier?). This time, however, I decided I needed to ask his holiness a more pressing question. I needed an answer to aid me in what I was dealing with at home. Wisdom that could only be imparted by the man who transcended Death as Gandalf the Grey, whose spirit traveled 'out of thought and time' to return reborn as Gandalf the White. Sure, it was a bit fantastical, but in the moment, it felt right.

Once it came to be my turn, I stood before Sir Ian McKellan, dressed in a smartly tailored brown tweed jacket and dark gray scarf. I told him I was caring for my passing father. I told him of the songs I sang to him with my sister and her guitar. I asked him based on his experience with his mother: "what else can I do to support him?".

He took my face in his palms and tilted his head to the side with a faint hint of tears in his eyes and said to me: "Just keep doing what you're doing. Sing him songs. Spend time with him. Tell him stories of your favorite memories together. You're doing just fine."

I broke down crying and he immediately held me in his arms. Gandalf and I embraced in tears. At that moment I felt like Frodo, held in Gandalf's arms with his staff in hand facing the Balrog disguised as the Grim Reaper. The flames beneath the bridge licking at our feet, and with a powerful stamp of his staff exclaiming "YOU SHALL NOT PASS!" to prevent the angel of death from taking me over completely in my grief.

And with that, I thanked him graciously and took my leave. Only now, I had the strength of the Maiar with me. I felt like a bonafide demigod wielding the Flame of Anor. An agent of the light rooted in goodness. Someone pass me my staff.

MUSIC AS MEDICINE:

Let Yourself be Moved

NAME OF THE TOOL
Music is Medicine
Let Yourself be Moved

BRIEF DESCRIPTION

Engage with music as your healer. It gets into places that your conscious mind can't.

SET THE CONTAINER

Seek out the healing properties of music. Have a dance party, pick up a drum, sing your heart out, pick up an instrument. Go for long walks with your headphones in. The song is on.

PRAYER /AFFIRMATION

I am free to be carried. Carried by Song, by Soul, by the Beat of this Holy Moment.

A mass migration of white cockatoos danced overhead toward their nightly den as I found myself on a swing in the outskirts of Sydney. I was so softly alone as the cool early spring dusk descended on the small Australian town I visited a month after my father's passing. On my large headphones blasted "Exit music (For a Film)". Catharsis personified. My life as a music video, orchestrated perfectly by Thom Yorke.

**"Breathe, keep breathing.
Don't lose Your Nerve"**
Exit Music (for a film) by Radiohead

Music tells a story and we all take liberties in interpreting just how the song is meant to be felt and understood though our own lenses. For as long as I can remember music has been my medicine. After being abandoned by my maternal family following a lengthy and tumultuous falling out, I turned to music as a young girl of 12. I would sit up at night, with my ear pressed to my radio, tears streaming down my face as the music illustrated how I felt. I was lonely yet not entirely alone. When Dad was diagnosed my relationship to my musical muse intensified. It was my teacher, my respite, my hype-man. When the emotions feel stuck and one is not sure how to process and release, music is there to tease it out.

All you need is a musical source, and a way to feel into the sound.

I began compiling a list of songs I could listen to while taking my long spliff walks in the early evenings while Dad sat at home with his head stitched up. The sensation of being amongst something so unfamiliar as illness and death was striking and I needed a way out, a way through, a way to process. Plus some time away from changing adult diapers was a welcome distraction. I called this playlist "Boohoo-utiful".

It was both beautiful and a window into a well of tears that stewed within me. Sometimes we all need that trigger and a safe space to let it flow! When friends failed to show amidst the chaos, I could be comforted by friends like Philip Glass, Ludovico Einaudi, Agnes Obel, Chopin, or Lady Gaga even.

Make a Playlist for Each Element

Think of yourself as a musical archaeologist. What tools can be used to brush the dirt off your bones and come to clarity of the deeper feels yet to be uncovered.

- **EARTH**
- **WATER**
- **FIRE**
- **WIND**
- **ETHER**

Or get abstract with it:

- The sound of two ferns brushing against each other in an old growth forest
- Water rushing over the river stone you picked up and put down
- The lives of water lilies bobbing on the surface of a pond
- The sound of liminal space
- God peeking through a storm cloud sky

Get emotional and compile tunes for certain feelings:

- Catharsis
- Freedom
- Bliss
- Contentment
- Horny
- Release

Practice putting together soundtracks to your life that feed a certain feeling.

Thinking of the journey we take as Hero(ine)'s of our own story it is helpful to have our own original motion picture soundtrack. The score of our lives. When you feel powerless, turn on your Super Hero playlist. When you need a space to crumple and dissolve, throw on some Nils Frahm. Find the music to color the personality of the archetype you are embodying that day. What special sound do you need to feel what you're lacking? What tune tells the story of your triumph, your sadness, your inner glow, that space within you that knows that through all this you will come out anew. Music is that gateway. The bridge. The place we can break down, build up, inspire, soothe, and comfort. Assemble your friends, press shuffle, and let spirit be the DJ.

NOW IS NOW:

Where else?

NAME OF THE TOOL
Now is Now
Where else?

BRIEF DESCRIPTION

Now. The IS-ness. Let's drop into it. Melt into it.

SET THE CONTAINER

Dropping into the now can sometimes be challenging. Suggestions: move that body, BB! Shake it out. Set it free. Dance it out until you can be still. You can stand up or sit in your chair and picture the sun coming from above and into your body, through your energy body, and down into your feet. You can then picture your feet growing roots, like an oak tree, anchoring your body into the above and below. In this space of groundedness you can be free of the fears of your mind, and are more able to enter the present moment.

PRAYER /AFFIRMATION

I ground into the earth. I pause and breathe. I am here to receive the present moment. I surrender to the Now.

"Get up, come on get down with the ISness"
sung to the tune of "Down with the Sickness"
by Disturbed

Here we are boys and girls, ain't no other time than now. The time is now. Now is the time. Now is the only time we will ever have. The past is gone, the future is yet to come. The only real moment we ever have is the present moment. And what a present! Gosh we sure are lucky. Every single moment we have a chance to completely reinvent who we are. We are not who we were even a moment ago. Who do we want to be now? And in the pain of sounding too goody two-shoes-esque, let's dive deeply into what a gift this present moment is. And how grounding it can be.

This truth totally tripped me out, y'all. It sounds super simple and for me it was HUGE. I was sitting in a cafe in Bali on my Griefcation® with a young American man named Ethan, who was tall, somewhat lanky, with short blonde hair and a dashing smile. We were speaking on the nature of reality. I was still very much in the space of grief, and quite spiritually tuned in. So tuned in, in fact, that I often had to pull over to the side of the jungle while driving my moped because I would be bombarded with what I call "spiritual downloads". They feel like an overwhelming data input that isn't necessarily words, though it can be, but feels more like a large chunk of wisdom that is being poured into the top of the skull like thick molasses. Yep. Probably wise to pull over to the side of the road. So as you can tell, my reality was very much … all over the place to say the least. So Ethan and I were chatting about the very fabric of reality over a vibrantly pink dragon fruit smoothie bowl. I was worried that first of all, I was definitely going crazy, and second of all, when would this end … and third of all, what does the future hold?

The grief I was feeling felt interminable. I felt like I would be here most definitely forever and that my suffering would never end. I felt panic over this. Utter panic, in betwixt amazing moments of clarity, epiphany, connection, and elation — between all that was panic. So much so that I would often nearly pass out from it as the world swarmed around me. Ethan explained to me this teaching from a dude named Eckhart Tolle. Now, I later found out this guy was so blasted off that literally one day he was so deeply and horribly depressed that his ego and consciousness literally shattered. He was blasted off into the ethers of enlightenment. Spontaneous enlightenment. Not only that, but the guy legit spent the next two years as a total loony toon sitting on a park bench in the middle of London, totally and completely blissed the eff OUT. I mean … what a trip! Now this guy is BFFs with Oprah and Deepak Chopra and has written a ton of epic books. One of which, *The Power of Now*, was gifted to me a short while after this conversation, by an equally blasty person who now goes by the name of "Blu".

Back to the conversation: Ethan tells me that all we have is right here and now. He talks about what Eckhart (bench dude) called: THE ISNESS. THE ISNESS of it all. Ethan cupped his hands face up as if he could somehow show the weightiness of all reality within his palms. It was all here for us. The reality-ish-ness of what our reality IS. The ISNESS encapsulates it all. It includes the here, the now, the past, present, future. I mean, heck, it probably includes parallel universes, and multiple realities for all I know! The ISNESS is ME sitting on a park bench in another universe that sits atop ours, completely blissed out, smiling ear to ear with not a care in the world.

The important takeaway here is this — all we have is now.

Cue "All We Have is Now" by the Flaming Lips

We are all: right here, right now.

Cue "Right here, right now" by Fatboy Slim

Now, I can't pretend to fully understand the wisdom behind the ISNESS, you'll have to check in with our boy Eckhart for that. Though for me there is a sense of comfort in it. That in a way, I don't have to have my hands so steadily grasping the wheel, white knuckling as I travel into the great abyss of the next moment. I don't have to worry about it. The ISNESS will take care of it all, because ... it is. And just to add a bit of a dose to your trip, let's just consider that not only does the ISNESS include all of our present reality, it also includes non-reality, dude! I know ... freaking wild.

So not only is there the ISNESS of this moment, there is the non-existence of it as well. Fullness. Emptiness. Simultaneously. And that is just great with me. In the same way there is ultimate good, love, connection, unity, there is the inverse: evil, hatred, disconnection, discord. We do not have to identify as one having more importance over the other. There is none. They simply are. They IS. So in the same breath we can say that we are both here, we are not, we are past, we are future, and we are not. Am I breaking your brain yet? Good. Mine too. Let's break it so we can break it open.

Listen: the moral of the story is the one mantra I used (and still do) to keep me grounded when the whole world was topsy turvy with grief and the idea of sitting on a park bench for two years was seeming more and more like the way to go. Put your hand on your heart, and repeat after me:

I am right here
I am right here
Right now
I am here

ONE FOOT IN, ONE FOOT OUT OF THE SPIRIT WORLD:

Creating Balance and Staying Sane

NAME OF THE TOOL

One Foot In, One Foot Out of the Spirit World
Creating Balance and Staying Sane

BRIEF DESCRIPTION

Everything Is In Perfect Balance. How to navigate balancing the inner and outer realms so you stay sane AND connected.

SET THE CONTAINER

Create a moment of sacred space. That could be intentionally, through lighting a candle or incense and sitting down to meditate, or it could be simply entering the eternal moment, here & now. In the midst of it all. It's so simple, it's that simple. It's that self-evident and that enduring, and that abiding. A few deep breaths will often do the trick. And now ... focus on dropping into your heart. Breathe into this sacred space of deep revelation.

PRAYER /AFFIRMATION

As I embrace everything I'm experiencing, I discover a deeper level of balance. I discover meditative moments that enhance my sense of peace. I make Gratitude my guide.

Hello dear one, I want to invite you to this new realm. Where you are not quite here and not quite there. A huge part of the process of being with the teachings that death has to offer us is the opportunity to straddle something vast and yet altogether simple. The veil between worlds exists all around us. We have only yet to see it and embrace it. The invitation here is to maintain one foot in the spirit world and one foot in what we call "the real world".

When I began my process of coming to terms with my Dad's diagnosis, I had a huge transformational experience. My sudden reality became something that was quite different than before, yet somehow it appeared to be the same from the outside. My perceptions of the world began to sharpen, and new senses turned on. Some may call this a spiritual awakening, though I try not to take myself too seriously! What can begin to happen as we engage with "death as a spiritual practice", is that these senses can begin to turn on. We have the ability to see beyond the veil of everyday reality.

Quantum physics tells us that between all matter is the tiniest matter that is dark matter. It is both infinitesimal and everything-immense-beyond at the same time. Dark matter comprises 85% of all matter. How cool is that! What they found when they were looking super deeply into the teensy-tiniest of atoms and molecules was that there was a whole lot of this stuff. The nothing. Apparently in every single atom, 99.99999% of it is made up of this nothing and the remaining .00001% is made of matter. Meaning, in a sense, that our reality is in fact, made up of mostly nothing. Or the space in between nothing. Trippy dude! I know. Have a little micro dose of that stuff. And be my guest, I am no astrophysicist but this stuff is cool and applies equally to the tiniest of bits of matter to the largest swaths of deep space. The research out there is phenomenal right now. They are finding more and more ties between science and spirituality (thanks deep space, let's re-enter the mystery)!

What this information tells me is further proving and shoring up my own experience. That the space beyond, the "other side" or "spirit world" as I like to refer to it as, is in fact, not that far away. If we consider that time and space is not linear, our understanding of what our world really consists of gets a bit ... sticky, so to speak. We can bring ourselves into the space of questioning, that allows us to come into connection with a sense of :

"There are more things in Heaven and Earth, Horatio, than are dreamt of in your philosophy."
William Shakespeare, Hamlet, Act I, Scene 5

That is to say that we cannot know for sure of much, though doesn't that present us with a wonderful opportunity to allow ourselves to straddle these worlds? If concrete is not actually solid, then what is? Seemingly nothing! Nonsensical, perhaps. But what an invitation! Let's dive in further.

Shamans over the ages have long been masters of this skill. Having one foot in, and one foot out. Straddling the world of the here and now, and that of the unnameable infinite expanse of the spirit world. By either imbibing hallucinogenic brews, smoking herbal allies, fasting for extended periods, or simply sitting in meditation: shamans, medicine keepers, sages, saints, and gurus of all kinds, lineages, and flavours have accessed this entry point. We can consider that if non-reality exists all around us, that all we must do is simply reach out and touch it to know it.

Why is this useful? To me it was particularly crucial in giving me the ability to be present with my father as he passed on. As I said, certain extra sensory abilities turned on around the time he was diagnosed. My world became ensconced in this level of thinly veiled perception particularly as he traveled between worlds during his coma preceding death. I sat by his bedside and entered deep, and long meditations, punctuated only by the slow inhales and exhales of my father. I was able to see where he was in his processing through my third eye visual perception. I saw that he was going through a sort of pre-death life review. I connected with the various helper spirits and guides that came to serve him.

This is what many call — The Liminal Space.

It is a juicy area of awareness where one might pierce through to see what is beyond the veil. I speak in perhaps vague terms because all of it really is up to the perceptor. Our own lenses and wisdom are the tools by which we enter in and interact with the unseen world, limited only by our openness.

Why is this helpful to the griever? Perhaps to give you solace. To know that if reality seems a bit askew, it is not your fault and it is normal. The fact that we pretend as a culture that death is as simple as going to the grocery store, and something to "get over ", to me signifies a failure to meet an epic opportunity. What if we gave ourselves permission to dive deeply into these liminal spaces? To see the sense of fear and not knowing —to really feel the EDGINESS of it all — and instead of shying away because it can be uncomfortable, to instead put on our shamanic lab coats, so to speak, and dive deeply into finding that space between spaces. That area between the fabric of our reality. To take the leap into the not knowing, beyond the veil. To see what is there waiting for us.

Here are a few practices I found extremely helpful while working in these spaces.

- **Nourishment is key. Keep yourself well fed with grounding foods:**
- **Root vegetables: potatoes, carrots, beets**
- **Warming soups**
- **Plenty of protein — you may find it easier to dive more readily into the spirit space by adopting a vegetarian diet during this though tune into what feels right for you. Some require that extra grounding that can come from eating meat. Find out what works for you.**

Keep the space energetically clear, uplifted, and vibrant:

- **Use sage, palo santo, or an essential oil diffuser**
- **Ring bells, clap your hands, or vocal tone to break the connection when necessary for yourself**
- **Place fragrant flowers in your area**
- **Play calming, angelic music (Gregorian chant, singing bowls, solfeggio frequencies)**
- **Create a crystal grid**
- **Light candles**

These tools can be used while working in the space of your passing loved one, or as a tool for yourself when diving into the work alone, or after their passing.

We have a special sort of VIP card when we are in this dance with death. An ability to more readily access this void, the liminal space, the spirit world.

PHONE A FRIEND:

Dial Into the Spirit World

NAME OF THE TOOL
Phone a Friend
Dial Into the Spirit World

BRIEF DESCRIPTION

Call upon the ancestors and notice the signs.

SET THE CONTAINER

First off: make sure your ancestors or any guide can take a trip into the light and thank you for it. Allies will be grateful - practice discernment. Think of it as a signal to noise ratio, and remember to fine tune the instrument (in this case your consciousness). You can program a bubble to not allow any energy not in the highest light and integrity to not be able to contact you or enter. In this way you set the scene for your beloved ancestors who are truly in service to your highest good to commune with you.

PRAYER /AFFIRMATION

I bow to my ancestors for all they have given me. I know that they are with me now. I embrace the teachings of my lineage as they come through. I fully receive this loving support. I feel their warm presence holding me, guiding me, helping me, healing me. Thank you.

Great news kids, you've been dialed straight into the best high-speed communication network known (and unknown) to man! Welcome to the wide web network of ancestors, guardian spirits, and helping entities. Woah, sounds heady, right? It is! Let's buckle up for a little ride along the high-speed-highway of light that is our network. Yes. That is right. Once your loved one has passed on, you (YES YOU) have access to this web of life. Lucky you!

One of the saddest things about losing a loved one (besides all the obvious sad things) is that we come to a point that is pretty darn trippy where we 'realize' that we can no longer pick up the phone and call them up. Weird right? Is this you right now? Pretty freaking wild, I know. Okay so here is the deal: yes it feels super strange to glance down at your phone and see their contact still saved there. Heck, maybe you even call them up, and hit their voicemail and WHOOSH there you are, sitting whilst crying profusely, as you hear their voicemail greeting. Tragic. So sad. This is shitty. But wait! What else can you do besides go through every voicemail they've ever left you while systematically demolishing every tissue box you own in your house? YES. That's right my

friends, you have the all access subscription to: PHONE A FRIEND
IN HEAVEN. Wooooo!

Psychics, shmycics. Here is the deal y'all. Here is the dis-
claimer, I have it on good authority that OCCASIONALLY a spirit
chooses not to hang around and they just blast off into the spirit
world and go on to do their learning for their next life so when
you dial them up you'll get a hella long busy tone or hold music.
That happens. I'm so sorry if that is the case with your loved one.
Though, my belief is 9 times outta 10 (these are good odds folks)
you can access your dearly departed! Now here is where we are
gonna get a little bit witchy (but you wouldn't be reading this book
if you weren't already, right)?

So here it goes: get comfy, find a nice place where you feel safe,
and held. Is it a power place? In nature? Or in the comfort of your
cozy bedroom? Maybe even light a candle. This is your intention:
I want to connect with my _____
(Insert name/relationship here) _____.
Add what you want: if a prayer feels right, say it … lean into
self trust.

Tune into your heart. Open fully to your heart space, because
this is how we are tapping into the network. Getting online is as
simple as one, two, three. Smile with your heart. You're in.

Offer yourself to the space that holds this communication.
Here is the opportunity to access your direct line to your beloved.
We have allowed this to come through for the benefit of you and
your loved one. Allowing the communication to come through so
that it all may be cleared. The fear. The doubt. The miscommuni-
cations that happened in life, what is unfinished, perhaps you need
help or guidance? Now is your opportunity. Sometimes we need a

helping ear to listen to, to cry to. Open yourself to speak out loud to your loved one. They can hear you. They are closer than you may think. Right there with you. This interweb is strong.

Ask for what you need. Courage? Stamina? Grace? Ask that they give you a message clearly so that you may understand. This may come to you as a smell, a vision, a word, or song that comes to mind, you may see your answer in life out in the world as a clue to your answer. Our loved ones have many ways of communicating with us. Spirit speaks in symbols. You may notice more of the animal that they identified with in life coming to you. Keep your eyes open as you go about your day. Do you notice certain numbers that remind you of them? Perhaps white feathers grace your path as you walk. Does that one red cardinal your mom always loved come by every morning and perch on the bush outside your window? How about the hawk that flies overhead when you are seeking support on perspective?

We can find these clues hidden in plain sight all around us. We must remain in a place of open hearted receiving. The lines never need close, unless you choose to. If it ever becomes overwhelming, you can simply ask for the guides to tone it down. Or if you need a complete break, ask them to turn it off for now. You can always tap back in when you are ready.

This access point also provides a pathway to connect to your other ancestors or guiding spirits. You may ask questions of them if you wish, or connect with one that you feel is aligned with your soul purpose. You will know when you meet them. I find it helpful at times to go into a deep meditation using shamanic drumming to easily and quickly guide myself into this interweb network of spirit. We all have our access points. Choose yours wisely. Practice discernment.

QUACK MEDICINE:

You Know, So Listen

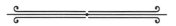

N AME OF THE TOOL
Quack Medicine
You Know, So Listen

BRIEF DESCRIPTION

Tune into your inner wisdom. You are your own teacher.

SET THE CONTAINER

Exploring alternative medicine is a wonderful gateway you may have already opened at some point in your life. Take it ALL with a grain of salt. Bring discernment to all that other people recommend. The "miracle" remedies. But stretch to expand what remedies you already have in your arsenal when it comes to homeopathy and the medicine of joy (dance, ice cream, etc). Listen to the niggles of intuition, follow them, and watch this line to your deepest knowing get stronger and stronger.

PRAYER /AFFIRMATION

Trust your knowledge when it comes to what you and your loved one needs. You are your best teacher and healer. Open to the medicine that you know is right for you.

This chapter is all about quack medicine. Meaning, yes, some of it can be thrown out in my opinion. Though as the saying goes, "don't throw the baby out with the bathwater!"

Here Is the Lesson: You Know Best

People with the best of intentions will come to you. Perhaps your loved one has just been diagnosed. They will have a large smattering of advice for you. They knew a friend who had the same disease ... and they were able to beat it just with wheat grass shots and cucumber water. Okay, good for them! I wish them all the best. Sounds like that bit of wisdom worked really well for them. Here's the thing. People will come to you with all sorts of advice, cures, salves, and healers to work with. This could be either for your loved one or for yourself. My advice here is to take it all with a grain of salt.

We all want something to hold on to — hope or a cure. These are both worthy things to wish for in times of need. And the truth is, within my belief system, there is a place for both. There is a place for the more esoteric and holistic practices, and there is a place for western medicine. I learned this the hard way when I had a nasty tooth infection that my holistic dentist was wary to actually admit needed a root canal. I went on for weeks during the pandemic in agonizing pain. I swear I saw God a few times. I tried everything: all sorts of tinctures, mouth washes ... flossing didn't help ... praying wasn't cracking anything. So finally I went to urgent care and my dentist had to listen up when the doctor said I needed opioid strength pain killers.

And I'll tell you something ... those shits WORKED. Much better than my tinctures and prayers. Not to demean the power of prayer which has been proven to immensely aid in examples shown by the Heart Map Institute and the work of Dr. Joe Dispenza. But I digress!

If the advice coming to you is for your loved one who is stricken by a disease of some kind, be aware. Trust your own inner guidance. Is this tool meant to help the person? If so, tune in and ask yourself if it will be of their highest benefit. Will they receive it in the way that will benefit their healing most?

Regrettably I fell prey to many people who were part of Multi-level marketing (MLM) and other get-rich-quick business schemes that promised the boast of vital health and wellness. "Just four pills a day of our ultra organic bio-dynamic green juice and fruit pills and your Dad will be cured of his brain cancer!" — Great.

We tried it.

Though it didn't do much to counteract all the steroid-induced binges he would go on. We'd find him in the kitchen at 2:00 am clad only in his tighty whities, face deep in a BBQ sauce-slathered rib bone. He was eating like there was no tomorrow because indeed, there might not have been one.

So be kind to yourself, be kind to your loved one. What is it that they really need most? Are they asking for treats? My vote is to give it to them, as long as it does not lead to more harm. Though this isn't your battle really. If they choose a certain route, allow them to take it. Again, this all comes back to intuition. We may be the most highly skilled healers, nutritionists, religious figures, etc., but when it comes down to it, if our loved one isn't open to whatever avenue of healing you're offering, don't push it. However painful it may be to keep your mouth shut. Believe me, I know. When I had learned in my research that cancer cells feed off of sugar, I tried my darndest to prevent my Dad from getting that next ice cream sandwich. The man had conviction. Who was I to say no?

Ice Cream: Pleasure Rx

I recall one particularly tragi-funny story. Everyday, the ice cream truck would come cruising lackadaisically around our neighborhood, as he had done since we were children. Mel, the ice cream man, would be ready for my Dad. He'd kindly serve my Dad his special treat that Dad accepted like an over excited toddler (because in many ways he was, with the brain tumor having changed his behavior). My Dad had really overdone it on all the treats after decades of stringent exercise and diet routines. One day Dad decided he wanted to improve his health, so he told Mel that no matter what, he was not to serve him any more ice cream sandwiches. Mel, knowing my Dad's situation, obligingly agreed.

It was mid-afternoon in early summer. Dad was peacefully napping in his bed. The melodic sounds of the ice cream truck approaching filled the house. He awoke with a start. He NEEDED that ice cream sandwich. He leapt up and hounded my mother for some ice cream money. Mom and I pleaded with him not to get any, reminding him that he'd given it up only days before. He was insistent. It turned into a scuffle. My Dad, all 6'2 of him, with a large steroid belly, clad only (as he often was) in his tighty whities, was wrestling with my Mom and me in the hallway leading to the front door. He managed to tear us loose and ran willy nilly into the street arms flailing in the air to flag down poor Mel.

Astounded by the sight (no doubt) of a 62 year old man in tighty whities appearing before his window, huffing and puffing, our dear Mel graciously gave in to my Dad's pleas. How could he not? With a shit-eating grin, Dad returned to sit on the porch, content with himself as white ice cream ran down the front of his protruding belly. This was his medicine. Turns out, what is best for us may not always be the most "healthy." If it brings us joy in the darkest of depths, I don't see any wrong in it. The space of pleasure and joy in itself is a medicine. That can be more medicinal than a green juice.

All this being said, I leave you with a final note. This is an invitation to not only choose and discern what may be "medicinal" to not only your loved one, but perhaps most importantly, to you. There are many alternative medicines and healing modalities that, in my belief, aid in our ability to process and mend. Systems I've learned to trust and value are Traditional Chinese medicine and Ayurveda. Partly because I've known their physical and herbal practices have helped me first hand, and also because they are systems developed thousands of years ago. I figure, if they worked for the sages living high up in caves, why couldn't they work for me too? Heh! But hey, don't take my word for it ... find your own medicine. You are your own guru!

"Quack Medicines" I know and love!

Herbs for grief:

- Cordyceps Mushrooms
- Eucommia Bark
- Reishi Mushroom

Herbs for anxiety:

- Ashwagandha
- Reishi Mushroom
- Peppermint Tea

Herbs for brain fog (grief brain):

- Turkey Tail
- Lion's Mane
- Schizandra
- Ginger/Turmeric Tea

Herbs for general recovery/immunity:

- Astragalus
- Chaga

Essential Oils

- **General stress relief:**
  - ◇ Lavendar
  - ◇ German Chamomile

- **Deep Breath Facilitators:**
  - ◇ Peppermint essential oil
  - ◇ Eucalyptus essential oil
  - ◇ Tea Tree essential oil

- **Grounding/Centering Scents:**
  - ◇ Frankincense essential oil
  - ◇ Myrrh essential oil
  - ◇ Cedar essential oil
  - ◇ Pine essential oil

Movement Practices:

- Ecstatic dance
- Five rhythms
- Qi Gong/ Tai Chi
- Walking
- Swimming
- Microcosmic orbit as taught by Mantak Chia

A note on discernment when looking for practitioners:

I have learned the hard way that we have to be really freaking meticulous when it comes to finding people that we invite into our homes, hearts, energetic spheres, and most importantly: our bodies.

Tip 1: Get a referral. Looking for a massage therapist, acupuncturist, shamanic practitioner? Ask around to your friends and groups. Who do they know love and trust? What do they have to say about them? I made the mistake of finding people via yelp reviews and rogue business cards on cafe's bulletin boards far too many times.

Tip 2: Carefully comb through their credentials. Take the time to read through what they're about. Who did they study with? For how long? What is their lineage? What is important to them? If you're about to sit with them during a plant medicine ceremony or have them pierce your skin with needles, you'll want to know they've done their due diligence and been properly trained. I can't tell you how many times I have heard of people going into sacred plant medicine ceremonies in some rando's backyard after a night of drinking having little to no preparation. Not only stupid, but potentially very dangerous. These practices are not silly little casual things. Healing (while at times can be so jovial and fun) is serious stuff. When we unlock deep seated emotions, memories, and funky juju we have to be very careful about the set and setting we are in.

Take it from our boi Terence Mckenna. What is the container? Who is taking care of establishing the energetic boundaries of the space? Is it safe and sanctified? Are you being respected? Will your body be respected throughout the experience? My wish for you as you continue on your healing journey is that you give yourself enough respect to take the time to find someone who you really resonate with. Even if it is just a yoga class! Just because you want to experience a certain medicine doesn't mean you should just go about it willy nilly. Find your peeps. Prepare appropriately. These healing lineages come to us through thousands of years of fine tuning and so it is imperative and our duty to treat them appropriately. Be respectful of the medicine you seek and find people serving it with integrity. Take it from someone who has kissed one too many frogs, y'all. Choose wisely.

RITES AND RITUALS:

Healing is Available to me Here and Now

NAME OF THE TOOL
Rites and Rituals
Healing is Available to me Here and Now

BRIEF DESCRIPTION

Align your chakras and balance your energy.

SET THE CONTAINER

Ground yourself into universal force by practicing your go-to grounding meditation. Calling down the sun, bring that blazing light down into your energy body, cleansing and purifying all in its path. When it hits your root chakra (where goddess Kundalini sleeps), picture it sparking off an immense explosion straight down into the center of the earth. Clearing any attachments and clearing your grounding cord of any disturbances. That explosion then comes back up and sparks a big explosion of light into your body, creating an egg-like circuit that you can *snap* into place once it's clear in your mind.

PRAYER /AFFIRMATION

I flood my energy centers with health and vitality. I find new levels of balance within and all around me. I open to the subtle healing that is available to me now.

After a person dies there is a strange sense of time. There is a feeling of "what now?". Everything has led up to this moment and now that they're gone there is a not knowing what to do next. There is nothing "to do ". There is loss, there is void, there is that moment between the exhale and in the inhale. Spaciousness. A very tender time that is incredibly special.

Dad died in the early morning. We spent time honoring his body, closing his chakras, laying yellow roses over him, taking photos and snipping off a lock of his hair (very Victorian!). After sitting in quiet contemplation, we called the hospice nurse and funeral home. As the funeral care directors packed up his body into a black body bag, I was playing with our cat Pandora in the backyard. She helped bring a sense of levity and joy to a very strange situation. We played till it was time to say goodbye beneath the mid morning sun, we stood around his body on our front walkway. Across the street roofers watched in quiet amazement as we said goodbye to his earthly shell. We joined hands around him then zipped up the body bag forever sealing into our memories what we knew of his hair, his face, his hands, his ears.

Then there was that feeling of ... what now?

I went back to our family friend's house where I had been staying part time. I laid down in the brass framed bed surrounded by pink flowered wallpaper, the sun streaming through the white lace curtains. I phoned my friend in Denmark via FaceTime. We spoke for a short while, her face beaming back at me with a smile surrounded by flaming red hair, a true viking woman. She offered soft words and a comforting ear as I recounted the glorious story of Dad's passing.

Then all of a sudden I felt something start to "happen". She could feel it too. A sense of birth? Of a shift? I couldn't put my finger on it. I told her "Hold on, something is happening". I closed my eyes and felt into it. My heart began to expand jubilantly. I felt around me a pouring over of some of the most unimaginable bliss and exaltation. I opened my eyes and saw that the entire room had been filled with golden light, cascading from the ceiling and down around the walls. Like a bright white and gold blast of heavenly bliss and joy. I knew at that moment my Dad had made it and he was sending a message to let me know all was well and he was happy where he had landed.

Wow! Even my friend in Denmark witnessing over our video chat was in awe. Again, not quite sure what had gone on yet we were astounded nonetheless. What can be said of that? Not much to be sure. I tell you this to let you know that magical moments like this are available. If you just pause and listen, and allow.

After Death Ritual and Care

This tool is one that I learned from the shamanic lineage of Alberto Villoldo, Author of *Shaman, Healer, Sage*. I studied this death rite ritual daily and carried the book from room to room with me while

Dad laid in his hospice bed in the living room. It uses the system of the chakras or energy centers and allows you to also honor and say goodbye to each part of your person.

Most recently I practiced it on the dead body of my grandmother who passed peacefully at the age of 98.

There is a gorgeous sense of peace being around a dead body, scary though it may seem. The first time I did this was on the body of my grandfather, Avi, who passed away a week before my father. It felt like a death & dying pop quiz! I'd been studying earnestly and here was my opportunity. His was the first dead body I'd ever been around which prepared me to be with my father a week later.

The basic system I use is inspired by the death doula I studied with and shamanic practices. Use what you will, and make it your own! There are many practices to draw upon and you may choose to use certain religious tools, songs, or prayers in your ritual. You may also want to discuss with your loved one beforehand and decide on what they want after their death.

Ritual Washing of the Body

Many cultures bathe the body post-death and there are intricate ceremonies that take place in order to prepare them. I will speak to the process I use which is less in depth than preparing for a home funeral which should be overseen by a professional death doula. Furthermore, there are certain religious practices that are also done outside of the home with designated practitioners. An example of this is the tahara, a jewish practice of cleansing, prayer, and guarding the body so the person can respectfully meet their maker, so-to-speak.

My process is a simple way to prepare the body for being taken by the funeral home, or undertaker, whoever that may be in your traditions. I find this is a good way of finding a connection with the process, while not having to do the more in depth processes that come with preparing a body for a viewing, or at home funeral and burial.

Options of tools to use:

- Holy water or flower water
- Crystals and/or power stones
- Candles
- Incense (frankincense and myrrh are lovely and bring a sense of sanctity)
- Flowers
- Washcloths
- Essential oils
- A bell or chime
- Sage or palo santo, smudge sticks
- Document the moment with pictures, video, sketching, whatever you're feeling

My process (choose what works for you and your loved one):

- **Moment of death:**
  ◇ Open a window so the soul may exit
  ◇ Ring a bell
  ◇ Celebrate! Do a Death Dance! They made it. Like the birth of a baby just in reverse. Dance your love for them. Dance for their courage. Dance your pain.
  ◇ Light candles or incense
  ◇ Smudge the room (this can be done anytime during the process)

- **Pause and breathe often:**
  - ◇ Notice the body
  - ◇ Allow for the liminal space to envelop you
  - ◇ Notice the stillness
  - ◇ Be here. Cry if you need to

Important to note, there is no rush to call the funeral home/hospice nurse/coroner to record the time of death. You may take all the time you need. Remember, they're not going anywhere! Enjoy these precious last moments with their earthly body

- **Fill a bowl with warm water:**
  - ◇ Optional: add holy water / flower water
  - ◇ Wet the washcloth: Lovingly wipe down their arms, face, legs, and hands, care for them like a newborn babe

Tenderly, tenderly. Breathe as you go

- **Arrange their body:**
  - ◇ Peacefully cross their palms over their chest
  - ◇ Straighten out their legs
  - ◇ Close their eyes or mouth

Important to note: go for progress, not perfection here. Dead bodies are sometimes difficult to maneuver so go with what is doable without having to crank them into specific shapes to look a certain way (just my 2 cents)

Remember, the death doula & funeral care team will have ways to secure their mouths and eyes so leave that up to them if you're doing a funeral viewing. We're going for the basics here

- **Place power stones/crystals on their bodies:**
  - ◇ Optional: I believe this infuses the power items with your beloved's wisdom and helps to balance the body's energies as you work

- **Hold their feet :**
  - ◇ Gently push and sway forward and back
  - ◇ This serves to expel the soul out of the body if any parts are lingering

You may sense the soul has already fully left the body though it doesn't hurt to give them a little extra push

- **Unwind and close the chakras:**
  - ◇ Beginning at the bottom, work your way up
  - ◇ Use the fingers or a stone dagger to unwind the chakras in the space above each center
  - ◇ Counter clockwise circles
  - ◇ Use your intuition to note when each center feels completely unwound
  - ◇ You may sing medicine songs or prayers as you do this
  - ◇ Completely disengage the soul from the body
  - ◇ Close off each chakra as you work your way up
  - ◇ Mark an X in the air above or whichever symbol feels right

A brief chakra guide:

- **Root** - perineum: center of basic animal needs (food, shelter, grounding)
- **Sacral** - below the belly button: sexual organs, womb center of creativity, sexual energy, watery emotions
- **Solar plexus** - below the ribcage: center of the will, self power, decision making center, the gut
- **Heart center** - the chest, heart space: love, compassion, relating to others, center of awareness
- **Throat chakra** - the throat: self expression, the voice, speaking personal truth, song
- **Third eye** - center of the forehead: intuition, connection to inner seeing, insight, vision, wisdom, psychic abilities
- **Crown chakra** - center of the skull (fontanel on babies): the space where the soul enters and exits the body. Connection to high states of consciousness, to the divine, ecstasy and bliss

On balancing your own energy centers:

It is especially helpful when doing work like this to make sure we stay balanced. We can use the method of winding up our chakras each morning or any time we're in need of an energetic tune up.

Ritual to practice:

Place a rose (real or imagined) in your palm

Starting from the top, make counter clockwise circles as if to soak up any negative juju from your aura and flick it off by sending it down into the earth or send into the open flame of a candle to be transmuted

Cleanse each chakra all the way down to your root using fire (visualization of fire)

To charge: starting from the top of the crown begin making clockwise circles and work your way down, infusing yourself with a sense of love, peace, and equanimity

Place the palms together and bow to your higher self, guides, and ancestors. Let your crown and soul shine. It is done!

SNACKS AND PANIC ATTACKS:

Nourish. Drop in. Tune in.

NAME OF THE TOOL
Snacks and Panic Attacks
Nourish. Drop in. Tune in.

BRIEF DESCRIPTION

Nourish your body in the now through mindful eating

SET THE CONTAINER

Get yourself a snack and gently acknowledge your surroundings. Eat slowly and with mindfulness, allowing this eating to be a meditative experience. An invitation to come back into your body.

PRAYER /AFFIRMATION

I ask for divine wisdom, courage, and strength. I find a safe haven in my body and in the present moment.

This is one of my favorite topics, y'all. Don't get it twisted, this one is huge. First of all, if you are having a panic (or anxiety) attack right now: get a snack.

Fave Snacks for panic attacks:

- **Almonds**
- **Potato chips**
- **Dark chocolate**
- **Miso soup with seaweed**
- **Cooked carrots**

Okay, you got your snacks? Good. Let's ground it down now, baby. You got this. Deep breaths. Find a safe space. If you're driving, pull over. Phone a friend if you can to let them know you're having a panic attack and need them to listen and help you breathe. REMEMBER: this too shall pass.

5, 4, 3, 2, 1 Grounding Technique:
(I did not invent this, just a tool I find works)

Say out loud:

- **5 things you can SEE**
- **4 things you can TOUCH**
- **3 things you can HEAR**
- **2 things you can SMELL**
- **1 thing you can TASTE**

Go ahead, do it. Yep. Out loud. You got this. Keep going. Need to cry? Let it out. Wail. Keep breathing. This will be over within a few minutes. You are alive and well. You are not going crazy. All is well. Keep your friend on the phone until you are back fully in your body and the panic has subsided.

Have another snack. Plan your aftercare.

Cancel the rest of your plans for the day and go home. For real. Call a friend to help you for the rest of the day. Have your friend prepare warm, nourishing, calming foods. Stay away from TV or phone screens. Listen to a gentle audio book or podcast. Have your friend read a storybook out loud as they feed you more snax. Put a weighted blanket on. Crank up the heating pad. Make yourself into a human burrito.

Many times I've had panic attacks during periods of my life when I was trying to be too many things, and solve all the problems, all at once. When I hadn't taken the time to process what had been going on emotionally in my life. I'd been stuffing it down and down and down until finally my body had to go ahead and have a breakdown FOR me, because I wasn't letting the steam out of my own pressure cooker gradually. You dig? This is why it is crucial to use the tools we have, of prayer, of meditation, of meditative movement, journaling, and the rest to give ourselves these times to let it all out. Otherwise the panic can set in like a runaway train. You're okay though, it is perfectly normal. To me, it is a sign that we need to do more self care, and nourish ourselves.

Tools for quick calm (I often carry one or two of these with me at all times when I've been in periods of more frequent attacks):

- **Herbs:**
  ◇ Reishi
  ◇ Ashwaghanda
  ◇ Mint tea

- **Essential Oils:**
  ◇ Eucalyptus
  ◇ Peppermint
  ◇ Lavender

- **Grounding Stones**
  ◇ Native American worry stones
  ◇ Obsidian
  ◇ Red Jasper
  ◇ Tourmaline

On a personal note, I want you to know if you are experiencing intense anxiety or panic attacks, you are not alone. Some find it helpful to work with mental health professionals to manage their experiences. For me, it has been most helpful to turn to the plant teachers by way of essential oils, hot baths, meditation, and making time each day for spiritual reflection. It won't be a one size fits all. If you are in crisis, there are a number of hot lines to help. I know deeply the feelings of helplessness and overwhelm that can result as a byproduct of grief.

I, too, have felt so in despair in moments that I did not wish for death but to merge with nothingness. To wish for a short reprieve from my reality. I encourage you to seek what feels the best for your care. I offer the tools that have helped me and I continue to navigate my own mental health, as I know we all do. Not a single one of us on this earth does not deal with some level of mental health struggles. It is normal. You are not crazy (important to reiterate)!

On a spiritual level, I've noticed I tend to have more panic attacks when I am going through a huge bit of change. When my psyche and spiritual essence are being upgraded in some way. When I am having new gifts turn on. Or when my gifts are screaming out for me to use them. Sometimes it can be hard to remember our strength and our own inner wisdom. Within us lie all the answers. My belief is that many mental health issues can be aided with long periods of time spent communing with nature. This is just my two cents, remember I am no professional. I share simply what my own experience has been.

There are shamanic teachers who believe that those with the more extreme cases of mental illness are perhaps our most gifted healers. That through our medical system they have been done a disservice. That their gifts must simply be recognized, nurtured, and protected in a safe space. They believe in the past these people would have been noticed by elders early on to have gifts. At such times they would be guided by a mentor to hone in on their psychic talents. This gives me some solace to consider. When I feel truly lost and exhausted by a particularly tough emotional time, I remember that help is always a phone call away. At any time I can call up my shamanic practitioner, my therapist, my friends, and having my animals around is always a huge help. As I write this I am surrounded by my sleeping pets: guardians of my writing. Space holders.

Finally I will leave you with perhaps one of my greatest teachers: the trees.

I had a moment during my anticipatory grief period where I sat in the backyard of my neighbor's house. Behind the outdoor lounge-set I was sitting on, stood an assortment of trees. Older ones, thick and rough with age, along with smaller saplings and teenage-looking trees. One might imagine a younger tree sprouting a small mustachio and defiantly nudging their siblings for more space to reach for the sun. As I sat there, with the early spring sun scattering through the leaves, I took a long notice of their branches, of their trunks. Of the leaves suspended above my head. I tuned into the trees completely. I understood one thing that I had known all along and yet somehow was now learning with new eyes. It may seem obvious to most and to me at this moment it was absolutely brand new.

The wisdom of trees is their patience. Their ability to stand still and all the while growing, slowly underneath it all, to the most infinitesimal degree that we cannot possibly see with the human eye. They're always growing. Staying still, grounded, and all the while growing up and up and up. Such wisdom! They did not boast! They did not show off, aside from their theatrical autumnal shedding of brilliantly colored leaves. They simply stayed put, patient. Swaying with the wind, in tune with their surroundings. Secretly passing nutrients to their brethren trees like sneaky classmates passing notes in school. The wisdom was in their silence. And I laughed. What good fun! What good teachers, how can I learn from them? What can I notice about their existence? Will they teach me?

A friend I'd met in Peru taught me how to talk to trees. Tarni stands over six feet tall, with long bronzed legs, and flowing blonde hair. A vision. A sort of tree-human. This Australian Amazon would teach me how to communicate with our tree friends. She told me of the lessons she'd partly learned from her Daoist teacher, Mantak Chia. This is my take ...

Tree Healing Exercise:

- **First and foremost, one must introduce oneself.**
- **Stand in front of the tree you'd like to interact with.**
- **Hold your hands up and to the side of your palms facing toward the tree.**
- **Notice how you feel. Can you sense the energetic field or aura around the branches?**
- **Has this tree been around a lot of humans in its lifetime? Or is it far off in the woods with only the woodland creatures as company?**
- **Smile with your heart.**
- **You may begin to sense whether or not this tree is down to hang.**
- **Some, you may be surprised, would rather be left alone!**
- **Listen carefully. Feel into their presence.**
- **Are they inviting you in?**
- **If you gain permission, you may slowly begin to walk toward your tree of choice.**
- **As you get closer, you may notice a shift within your energy already.**
- **Once you arrive. Place your palms to the tree, if you get the go ahead, I highly suggest getting your full belly pressed up against the tree. Embrace your inner tree-hugging hippie.**

- At this moment you may choose what it is you wish to receive from the being.
- Do you need grounding? (often after an intensely emotional time I ask for this)
- Do you need wisdom?
- Do you need perspective?
- Do you need a hug?
- Do you need peace?
- Do you need a friend?
- What can you give?
- What do you offer this magnificent being?
- You may choose to spend a little or a lot of time with your new tree-friend. You can always return for more chats at a later time.
- Thank them for their time, perhaps bow to them, and be on your way

TRAVELLING SHAMAN TOOLKIT:

Assembling Your Tools and Creating Sacred Containers

NAME OF THE TOOL
Travelling Shaman Toolkit
Assembling Your Tools and Creating Sacred Containers

BRIEF DESCRIPTION

Upgrade and/or refine your ceremonial toolkit. Make an altar in your home. Select basics that can come with you to create a home altar wherever you go.

SET THE CONTAINER

Gather together a bundle of power objects including crystals, sage, palo santo, incense, Himalayan salt. Now you can stop, drop, and connect with your Self whenever you need to!

Clean (physically) and clear (psychically) your space. You can cast a circle of white light and throw in St. Germain's violet flame (ask and thank St. Germain for his blessings). Create a sacred altar space in your home. Fill it with objects and photographs that honor your ancestors and spiritual teachers. If you already have an altar, rearrange or clear that sacred space.

PRAYER /AFFIRMATION

I CREATE and CONTAIN sacred space with ease and grace.

When I first began creating an altar space I had no idea what I was doing. Really. I was not raised in a religious household and so when I pulled a goddess card deck soon after my Dad was diagnosed that told me to "create an altar", I was vaguely aware of where to start. The Celtic goddess Nemetona on the card seemed to give me permission to acknowledge that what I was going through was indeed spiritual and that I would need an area in my home to honor that.

My Dad wasn't religious either, though he claimed to be a Methodist. He had gone to church with his southern grandma in Texas as a kid and knew a bit of the bible. Nevertheless, we didn't have anywhere in our home that was sacred. We had bookshelves filled with knowledge of the arts, travel, cooking, and architecture. Along the shelves were small tchotchkes my mother collected. The statue of liberty, an astronaut, small lego figurines. Sure, these were items that brought joy to my mother at least, but was it sacred?

Eager to create my own sacred space I turned to my friend, Sparrow, who was most definitely a witch. She had told me of her travels in South America studying with a shaman, giving a sort of foreshadowing to my future endeavors. I had stayed over with her a few nights and learned from her. She had a low table, close to the floor, alongside were cushions to sit on. Along its dark mahogany surface were several colorfully woven cloths upon which laid crystals of all shapes, colors, and sizes. I had never known what a crystal could be used for, other than decoration. She and I smoked a small amount of marijuana and she allowed me to hold one of her beloved crystal tools. I could feel energy pulsing through my palms.

There seemed to be a characteristic of this cold stone warming up in my hands. Like it had a personality. She lit a large stick of wood that filled the room with the most wonderful and intoxicating aroma. "Palo santo", she told me, was the name. Waving her arms through the air, allowing the sumptuous smoke to saturate the space, she told me of her shaman. Of these large bonfires he would light at night during their plant medicine ceremonies. The palo santo was in large supply and he would load up the pyres with stacks of the aromatic wood. I was bewitched.

We sat quietly next to this space which was more and more seeming like a portal as I allowed myself to relax in its presence. I gazed upon the artifacts as Sparrow lit the candles one by one, with the careful attention of a zen Buddhist. Each moment was carefully choreographed with seeming ease. A dance of the sacred. I looked at the candlelit items. Photos of masters sitting in the lotus position. Seashells collected with care. A starfish. An obsidian angel. The items were arranged in a way that suggested order. A sort of grid, if you will. I noticed how I felt in front of the grid. It seemed to align with me. It was an entry point. Yes, I knew now it was a portal.

Determined to make a portal for my own use, I set about gathering objects that felt powerful. In my room, I cleared out a shelf atop a small bookcase and with carefully laid out chosen tools. A black and white photo of my father as a young man, sitting on cousin Bobby's Piano bench, with her parrot Sylvester perched atop his shoulder. Next to that I laid out a cloth and chose a few rocks and crystals I had collected over the years. One I had chosen from the stream bed at our family's country house in the Catskill Mountains of upstate New York. A clear quartz crystal I had been gifted by a yoga student in the shape of a heart. Some shells I had collected from the beach of my hometown on the Long Island Sound.

A portrait of our Norwegian forest cat Hercules who had passed a few months prior watched over the scene. A sort of guardian angel now. I lit a few candles and sparked up a few leaves of dried sage. The senior yoga teachers at my studio were always burning the stuff, and some ornery customers would walk in complaining: "it smells like marijuana in here!" I never minded. Sparrow had taught me that sage can be used to cleanse and clear spaces, people's energy bodies, crystals, and stones.

There are many kinds of smoke that can be used in this way, I've come to find out over my years of study. Juniper, sweet grass, or tree resins like copal, frankincense, and myrrh. Find what works for you. Yes of course there are the detractors who warn that one is appropriating a culture by using certain smoke varieties. My belief is that if done with intention, and gratitude for the plant and its wisdom, one cannot go wrong. It is all about intention. We cannot go wrong if we are within alignment of our true selves.

Here is the tool y'all: make your sacred altar. Whatever floats your boat goes. What is calling to you right now? Are there any figures or deities that call to you in particular? I love working with the goddess Kali (though she is fiery and one must be careful), my other faves are Tonantzin, Archangel Michael, Metatron, Lahiri Mahasaya, and more. I change around the photos I keep on my altar depending on what energy or wisdom I'm working with. Surround yourself with items that speak to you in a powerful way. Make it nice. Find the way of beauty through this practice.

It is sweet to arrange a bouquet of flowers to sit atop your altar space. We are making a practice of inviting in sweetness and sanctity. You may choose to find a ceremonial cloth that works for you. While some may opt for one that is intricately woven with prayers, you can also keep it simple and lay down a scarf you enjoy. Where attention goes, joy flows. Within different lineages, there may be a certain order you choose to place your items. Allow yourself to choose what feels good to you. My prayer for you is that you give yourself permission to create a space that is sacred. A place where you can come to for respite. A place to connect with the divine. For your guardians and ancestors to hear your prayers. A place to forgive, to cultivate compassion. Ram Dass famously placed a photo of Donald Trump on his altar space to represent someone he had a hard time finding love for. A nice idea! It is your working space. It is a safe space for you. It is yours. Your portal. Your altar. And so it is!

Now it's your turn. These are the steps in setting up your altar:

Things to collect:

- Photographs of ascended masters
- Shells
- Candles
- Feathers
- Power stones (great to collect from a Power Place)
- Crystals
- Tchotchkes that remind you of your soul essence

Ancestors altar:

You may also choose to make a special spot where only your ancestors will live. Some find it helpful to keep it in a sort of menagerie that you open and pray to at the beginning of the day, and close at night with your evening meditations.

- Photos of your passed loved ones
- Pics of your pets who have crossed over the rainbow bridge
- Rainbows! The gateway to the beyond
- Family mementos
- Their fave drinks/candies/foods (change frequently so things don't get moldy!)

A month after Dad passed I found myself in a Wachuma ceremony in the Byron Bay hinterland of Australia. Sitting with the long white-pink-and-purple-haired South African curandera I had met while in Peru, I was surrounded in a circle by magical beings. Human and otherwise. I went deep into the medicine on that journey. A cat I had visioned prior to the medicine circle mysteriously appeared right on time and laid with me for the first few hours as I contemplated forgiveness. Later in the afternoon, the cat signaled to me it was time to shift in my learning as it got up to stretch and yawn beneath the large tree canopy that watched over us. I went on to bathe naked in pools of crystal-laden waters.

The lush forest surrounding us seemed to be alive with mythical creatures. I swore I saw centaurs, elves, and the Greek god Pan peering through the leaves. After a deep conversation with a tree stump contemplating death, I moseyed my way back to the circle. I noticed a group of fellow journey folk gathered behind the house. In front of them was laid out the most wonderful collection of crystals, shells, amulets, and leaves, and feathers. All perfectly arranged in a way that beckoned one to come closer. At the base of the grid was a single leaf. We gathered in front of it. One of my fellow journeyers exclaimed, "it is a portal!" and we knew it to be true. The entire configuration of power items had been carefully curated to become a vortex-like portal through which people could travel. I came to understand at the moment, how these types of altars could be assembled.

When going into battle, every warrior must have their tools. Their shield, their sword, their armor, and that special magical talisman that brings them good luck. Think of tennis players who have to wear that lucky sock when they go against their opponent. You know the drill. This is you now. You, too, need your own special tool kit. You will bring this with you wherever you go, where it feels necessary. The elements of a basic tool kit will come in handy as you go through this process. You will bring this traveling toolkit with you when you go to a new place, if you are going through your Griefcation®, or if you are going to do meditation or practice with a friend on a mountain top, it is also handy there.

We bring this with us as a special satchel to go into the world of spirit. So when we have our morning and evening prayers, this will be there for you. When you need something to ground down and feel you are going insane, this can have your back. Every medicine carrier has their own set of tools. Feel free to augment and shift into what resonates best for you. What I include here is simply my basic list of what I think is most helpful. You are your own guru, so choose what works for you.

ULTIMATE FORGIVENESS:

A Willingness is Enough

NAME OF THE TOOL
Ultimate Forgiveness
A Willingness is Enough

BRIEF DESCRIPTION

Enter the sacred space of willingness to forgive.

SET THE CONTAINER

Drop in and set the container that brings you a feeling of safety and support. This could be lighting a candle, casting a circle, lighting incense, and generally supporting yourself with coconut water, water, blankets, pillow, and tissues. Rose quartz is a great ally for this work.

PRAYER /AFFIRMATION

I lean into the tenderness of the complex feelings I have for those who I harmed and those I have harmed. I set the intention to forgive myself. Forgive the past. Forgive everyone. I give all challenges and misunderstandings over to the great force of Divine Love.

Forgiving Your Loved One

Dad was accused by my cousin of molesting her at a young age. This sucked. A lot. The accusation came out during her teenage years after my cousin had gone through multiple treatment centers for depression, many mental health professionals, and a pharmacopoeia of drugs. I do not say that to diminish her credibility. This has been a long road and even talking about it now is super tender and vulnerable. This story is one I normally share with a close and trusted friend after a bottle of wine or two.

I'm writing this and I face so much resistance in telling you my truth. I am going to keep on writing because this is hard. I have twenty minutes to write and here I am. I am writing about forgiveness. I have learned a lot about forgiveness and have gone through many different utterances of what I believed it to be.

I had a deep dive into understanding what it was at a young age. After losing my family due to this accusation I had to try to understand at the young age of 12 why I could be abandoned by the very people who were entrusted to guide me through this life.

They were simply not there anymore. How could I forgive my cousin for tearing apart my family? For skewing my perception of my father. And even now, as he is gone five years from this earth, this accusation still paints the reality of my interactions with my aunts as we carefully comb through the house my grandparents lived in. My grandparents cut my mother out of their will and so I am now tasked with keeping their belongings. Which means I have to go through it all with my aunts. People who I had not seen for 20 years and loved so dearly. It is incredibly painful and so I am working still with compassion and forgiveness.

What I find to be so fascinating about forgiveness is its nuance. You see, there was never any real evidence against my father. He was a family man. He came home from work each night and was at the table for every dinner. He helped my sister and me during bath time and played his classical guitar for us as we fell asleep.

My cousin had been having nightmares during her stay at a residential mental health institution following a suicide attempt. She relayed these nightmares to her caretakers. She explained stories of visions during these nightmares of being penetrated. She did not know by what. Slowly over the course of her treatment, she began to see this person as being my father. A recovered or repressed memory is what the experts called it. And with that, the witch hunt began.

What started as a nightmare fully transformed into a real-life terror that played out before our eyes as if in slow motion. The accusation. The police reports. The sheltering of my sister and me against this rumor. The slow dissolution of our family. A once strong family of immigrants from Spain. A large and culturally rich extended family. Intelligent people. My grandparents spoke over three languages each. How could they all believe this?

The issue was that because this was a nightmare there was no "truth" to go on. There was no evidence of her having been abused at the time she said she was. And what's more is that my sister, other cousins, and I had never been abused either. As the young woman I was becoming I remember wracking my mind once my mother had told me what my family believed. I tried with all my might to uncover some memory of my father doing something like that to me. I tried because if I could uncover some deep-seated memory to prove this horrible thing about him, it would mean I could get my family back. My mother's family had given her an ultimatum. They said, "your husband is guilty of this. Either you divorce him or you never see us again".

On the morning of September 11th, 2001 I was playing the flute for my symphonic band in seventh-grade middle school. I was called out by an aide. My mother was waiting at the school office for me, a worried look in her eyes. She told me "there has been a bomb in New York City". I asked if Dad was okay, she assured me he was, though she herself had no way of knowing whether he had made it. His office was downtown.

We packed my bag and drove up to the high school where my sister and cousin Paulie waited outside. Together we drove home, past the bay. Across that clear blue September sky over our hometown waters loomed a large black dust cloud. This was what movies looked like. Over the car radio, we heard the announcer speak the words "the second tower has just fallen."

We sat together in our living room, all three of us munching on the snacks we had packed for school that day. My mother frantically assembled go-bags for us. She was preparing for the worst. We heard a knock at the door. It was her sister, our Aunt. I could overhear a hushed argument between them. Tita Catherine entered the room. "Paulie, it's time to go". She yanked him up off the floor and carried him out as scenes of the tower collapse played on the television in front of us. This was not just a collapse of our world as we knew it. The whole world lost something that day. As the towers crumbled, so did my family. Over an ambiguous nightmare.

I watched a documentary when I was 15 about the Jews of Nazi Europe and how their beliefs in forgiveness lay with them all these years after the holocaust. A rabbi from Jerusalem spoke about the importance of forgiveness. To him, there was a threshold. A point of no return. A point after which no forgiveness could be offered. Something that to many is viewed to this day is absolutely unforgivable. The forced concentration camps, the executions, the murder in the public eye of so many innocent men, women, and children. So what did the rabbi say? He told Germany as a nation that soon their time for forgiveness would be up. That to him, it had a time stamp. Luckily for the nation of Germany, in a constant state of self-flagellating: "mea culpa", it offered a diplomatic apology to the people of the Jewish faith. They accepted it, having agreed that it was within the time frame of allowed for forgiveness.

I loved this idea. To me, the time frame was up. But I learned that life is not that simple. You cannot *force* someone to apologize for something of which they feel no remorse. You cannot force guilt and shame. So what happens? How do we confront those inner demons that tell us that some of those who have wronged us are forever wronging us? That without an appropriate apology, we cannot move on? When do we realize that the pain of their hurt over and over again cannot live in our memories? It is only hurting us to hold on to it.

We choose to forgive when the pain of holding on is more than the pain of letting go. We forgive others to forgive ourselves.

Forgive ourselves for being so hurt. For reacting in the ways that we did. For saying the awful hurtful things hurling insults at others either in real life or in the hellscape of our minds. For taking out the pain and betrayal on ourselves. For the self-harm, The late nights drinking and chain-smoking. The tears spread long and far along rivers worldwide. Glancing up at the moon asking "why?" You deserve this peace. It is hard, I know. But what we come to when a person is dying is a grand opportunity.

Was your loved one a saint? I venture to guess that they were human. Flawed. Nuanced. Human. They made mistakes. They lacked understanding and acceptance when you wanted love and affection. You were hurt by them just by the matter of life. That within the experience is suffering. It is imprinted. We go into relationships in life knowing that we will be hurt and we will be the cause of hurt. So what then?

Forgiveness as I have come to understand it is a lifelong process. A turning over and over like the tilling of soil. A new memory surfaces, even long after they're gone and you think: "my god, I thought I already worked through this?". But no, there is yet more to forgive. More to release to the land, the sky, the heavens, to their memory.

We never stop forgiving. Ourselves and others. It is the best option I feel. I am no expert but I know as I continue to turn toward love and forgiveness I heal myself. To hold that anger and resentment only hurts me in the end. And to forgive does not mean that the person has to be a part of our lives whether living or dead. We choose to forgive to grant ourselves grace.

They do not have to be sanctified or martyred in our memories. They do not have to suddenly become a trusted lifelong friend once more. We can choose to love them for the lessons we learned. For the ways in which we became harder, more tough, more resilient. For who we became when we turned our light away from the world and went into our own journey. For how we learned to protect and create boundaries. But what is perhaps more important is that in forgiving we open a window to allow a breaking down of those patterns. A rebirth, of course. Because what other option is there? A hardening until complete calcification? Until we are sat alone in a padded recliner surrounded only by painful memories, and a hardened heart. Ornery. Curmudgeonly. How dull! Hard pass.

Instead, we can offer the allowing. I forgive to heal myself. All things in my eyes are forgivable. Perhaps the more "unforgivable" acts are even more ripe and ready to dissect and find beauty in. The ones who are international persona non gratas. Them too. Because in my view all of us are just permutations of the unnameable. Consciousness experiencing consciousness. God creates to live and see itself in all things, including the ugly. Including the blood-red rage, the disgusting, and those strange creatures that seem to have no purpose.

Ticks for example! Or possums, those horrible looking things. Yes, them too. Perhaps serving no other purpose than to bring about the contrast of fear and disgust. The universe just says yes to all. And to invite that YES into our hearts and hold that too. Huge. Powerful. Transcendent. Hard, no doubt about it. But more easeful than the alternative. A suggestion with a wink of my eye, lovers.

So what have I forgiven? In the end, I forgave my father. I had to forgive him for both realities. The reality that said he was a child abuser. I let myself dive into that reality completely during one of my ayahuasca journeys. I asked to be shown what I feared the most. I was shown the abuse. I could see that it was possible. I could see that he could still be my father. I could still love him even with this potential reality. It broke my brain and heart completely wide open. On the other hand, I had to learn to forgive my family. They believed fully that my sister and I were under the care of a child abuser. They lived their lives each day in their homes not but 5 minutes from our own for over twenty years believing in their hearts that my sister and I were in the home of a sex offender. What adult leaves a child with someone they believe is a monster? I wonder sometimes if perhaps this was their own doubt.

For me, I think of children I know and love. How I would scream and shout and tear down the doors of any home I believed they were in that was unsafe. But my family lacked courage. I can forgive them for this. I can forgive them for dwelling in their gray zones of clouded comfort. Because at the end of the day, I learned how to love myself. I learned to forgive myself for all the ways in which I had barred my heart. For the years I spent thinking I was somehow disgusting, discarded, and unlovable. Congratulating myself on each small victory that shows I can heal from this monumental wound.

Recently in conversation with my aunts, while sifting through my grandparents' antiques, they pleaded with me to just come to their side. See it from their point of view. My father was a monster. A sex fiend. A man with no remorse. A sociopath perhaps even, in their eyes. I tried. I said to them: I believe my cousin. I affirm her experience. I believe my father could be capable of something like this. And I believe my father could be innocent. He maintained his innocence until the day he died. They could not appreciate this feat of mental and emotional dexterity. I am reminded of the quote by F. Scott Fitzgerald that says "The test of a first-rate intelligence is the ability to hold two opposed ideas in mind at the same time and still retain the ability to function." To them, this wasn't enough. They gave me the same ultimatum they'd given my mother years before. I paused, got very still. And chose. I choose me. I forgive you, and I choose me. I choose my ambiguous truth. I will not remember my father as a monster. I will remember him for who he was. The good, the bad, and the ugly. That is enough for me. It wasn't for them. And that is okay.

This serves to say that we can love people and accept that they are flawed. That we are flawed. That we are trying our best. We can hold people accountable for their misdeeds, surely. Though how can we bend ourselves to show mercy? Mercy to our own hearts. Mercy to those who wronged us. Mercy to those godforsaken ticks!

Forgiveness around death is crucial. As the portal opens for death to peek its head in and transform our lives, we are given this opportunity. To see forgiveness through. Many believe that souls carry on to finish taking care of any unfinished business until they depart. With this in mind, I went to my grandmother's bedside as she prepared to leave her body.

My Aunts, mother, and sister, and I were gathered around Abuelita's bed for the first time in over 20 years. Her mind had gone but her spirit was strong. She gazed up at all of us with one moment of fleeting clarity, looking deeply at each of us. Her mouth hung open. After all the years of heartbreak and tumult. To have all her daughters together in one room once more. To have her granddaughters there. Forgiveness.

Forgiveness can happen in the words between. In the space of willingness to be there. No words of the rift were spoken. Simply, we stood as the women we had become around our dying matriarch. In astonishment, Abuelita remarked: "magnificent!" Eyes ablaze in wonder.

My belief is that if we grant our loved ones forgiveness, we ease their souls a bit. Ours too. A soothing. It can come before or after the loss. Time knows no bounds. Forgiveness can come in waves. One day you are fully on your knees humbly offering forgiveness and the next a sweep of resentment comes through town putting you into a spitting yelling fury. And still, we come back. We breathe into it. We scream into it. We slowly unravel those parts that are filled with guilt and shame and hatred. We curse the stars. Then slowly, slowly we come back. Another layer. Forgive, forgive, forgive. Because the other option is what? Hold on? Kill your own spark with this hatred? To me in the end it ain't worth it.

I think back to that day in September when so many lives were lost in New York City. When the perpetrators of this act were elusive. When the anger had no outlet. What did the city do? We cared for each other. We found ways to console. To hold one another. We used music, art, poetry, and comedy to soothe those places in our hearts that begged for retribution. For meaning. How could something like this be forgiven? Yet we found a way. And we continue to. So to me, forgiveness is perhaps our greatest teacher. One that shows up time and again as an opportunity. To melt and break and grow a little bit stronger. Ultimately forgiven, ultimately forgivable, ultimately forgiving.

So when I think of my family and my cousin specifically, now I hold love for them in my heart. I can come to the Buddhist Metta Loving Kindness prayer:

May they be happy
May they be well
May they be peaceful
May they be free
If I have hurt anyone, knowingly or unknowingly in
thought, word or deed, I ask for their forgiveness.
If anyone has hurt me, knowingly or unknowingly in
thought, word or deed, I extend my forgiveness.
And so it is.

VICES:

Letting Go of Rigidity

AME OF THE TOOL
Vices
Letting Go of Rigidity

BRIEF DESCRIPTION

Permission to do that naughty thing (in moderation!).

SET THE CONTAINER

Create self-trust amidst the indulgences by taking the time for mindful use. Get the good tobacco. Make a ritual of use if it is something ongoing. Say a prayer every time you light up. Have a special chalice. Sky's the limit.

PRAYER /AFFIRMATION

Now is the time to get a little wild. Nourish yourself with pleasure. Let its joyful qualities heal you.

Take a break from your whiskey and coke and put out that cigar for just a moment so we can have a very serious discussion about VICES. And by serious I mean, not really that serious at all, ever, because life is meant to be lived and celebrated. Here's the deal. You have just been dealt one of the roughest freaking hands of life experiences of all time. Legitimately. There is no way to sugarcoat this besides the generic "find the silver lining" stuff. For those who are in recovery or struggle / have struggled with addiction ruling your life, a lot in this chapter isn't for you, babes. Especially not if you don't have a support system to lovingly check on you when you need it. Some of it is. Cue Netflix and your favorite indulgent foods. You are responsible to know what to take and leave here.

Whether you've recently received the terminal diagnosis of a loved one, or a beloved soul has dropped dead for any absurd and tragic reason, I'll tell you straight off the bat: you're gonna want to grab something to ease the pain. Here's the good news: that is perfectly o-freaking-kay. Okay? The thing about dealing with this whole "death" stuff is that, yes, it is some pretty heavy business, and we all find ways to cope differently.

Here are your options, but feel free to get creative with the subcategories:

- **Food:**
  - ◇ Candy/chewing gum, snacks

- **Media:**
  - ◇ Social media, television, Netflix

- **Alcohol:**
  - ◇ Wine, beer, liquor, kombucha

- **Tobacco:**
  - ◇ Cigars, rollies, ceremonial tobacco

- **Marijuana:**
  - ◇ Hash, edibles, dabs, etc.

- **Caffeine:**
  - ◇ Americano, espresso, yerba mate, matcha, chocolate

- **Sex:**
  - ◇ Take a lover, buy some fun toys for your own exploration

Now here is where I'll draw the line. At no time will I advocate for the use of narcotics of any kind. That's the thing y'all. No crazy stuff that you'll get insanely addicted to leaving you in a worse place than where you started. If you're already using and need support, do not hesitate to get the help you need. Your life depends on it. Seriously.

The vices I've listed above are 100% Elena's Grief Force regimen approved.

This is why: Vices help to give us the time and space to really process things. Sure they may not be the "healthiest" things in the world but hey, you're grieving for crying out loud! When Dad was first diagnosed I developed a very intimate relationship with my friend "Le Spliff". He was a fancy french rolled cigarette sprinkled with my good friend Mary Jane. I would creep away for a little bit of "me" time, lock myself in the basement bathroom, turn the fan on, light an incense stick, spark my little friend, put my headphones on, and just tune in/tune out. Afterward, I'd take a long sad walk to the water, listen to my playlist called "Boohoo-utiful" and cry it all out. Definitely wore sunglasses at night to shield passing cars from my obvious despair. They probably thought I was insane, I didn't care.

Escapist? Sometimes. I will admit, all the vices are ways to either tune in to your 'suffering' or tune it out. Either way, you're going to go through it. What helped most about having a relationship with marijuana was that it enabled me to engage in a deeper connection with myself. Humans have turned to medicinal plants, spirits, and other creature comforts for eons and I believe there is wisdom in that. Instead of punishing or shaming ourselves for needing to take the edge off, can we learn to embrace it mindfully?

For me, I came to understand there were times when I needed to be totally stone-cold sober as a nun. When I knew that I could not touch a drop of alcohol for months and years at a time during this process. I knew that if I were to bring that spirit into my sphere it would disorient me in ways that would not be helpful. Especially when the veil between worlds was very thin I needed to be as grounded as possible. Spirits can be used to create mind-altering atmospheres which can either help us to get closer and find connection to others and the heavens or if used in certain ways it can drive us further away from connection. Benjamin Franklin is credited for having said "Wine is constant proof that God loves us and likes to see happy." I agree with Ben!

Occasionally it can be a jovial bringer together or people, hearts, and merriment. And there is a fine line when that can descend into darkness. Both have their merits and uses. Bawling while singing drunk karaoke on our living room floors is perhaps just as cathartic as dancing a group jig in the local saloon. It is our job to decide when and how we choose to imbibe.

What about the saying "everything in moderation, including moderation"?

Thinking back to a time in my life just a few months before Dad went into hospice. I was still living in Brooklyn and in that state of unsureness that comes with the territory of anticipatory grief. No idea when or how he would go, a vague idea, a fog of dates and prognoses. I had savings to live off of and didn't want to take a job in case I got that call which at that point could really come any day. The call to say "it is time to come home".

During the day I was either in deep meditation, spending time smoking tobacco with the plants on our large outdoor deck garden facing the New York City skyline, crying in our outdoor rooftop shower, or dressing up to creepily stand on the corner a block away and watch Tina Fey direct a comedic TV show. Ya gotta do whatcha gotta do, ya know? It was a lifestyle of listlessness.

One day I got a call from my Danish friends saying two of their incredibly good-looking architect friends would be visiting

Manhattan and would I show them some hospitality with a tour of the sights. Well, who was I to say no? What ensued was a couple of weeks spent with these two figures of male adonis-hood. Just visions of a Viking pleasure cruise. As life was still in the threshold of neither here, nor there I embraced these new friends fully. Each day was spent gallivanting around the city with these tall blonde Danes, smoking imported cigarettes, drinking beers, having the occasional spliff. We were living. Sure, I was taking the edge off a bit but I felt instinctively I wouldn't get this chance again for a while.

One night I visited them at their flat which was in one of the oldest and first skyscrapers ever built in New York City. This thing was magnificent. Old stone facade. Inside was the makings of an abandoned old school bank, long forgotten by time, though singing the echoes of dead Rockefellers and Astors. I was in architectural heaven. This place reeked of old New York. We snuck up to one of the higher floors and the boys navigated me through what looked like an old steam ship's engine room. Bobbing in and out between two-foot-wide white pipes we found our way to a window that led onto a ledge overlooking all of Manhattan. We cracked open a few beers and lit up some cigarettes. The view absolutely took my breath away.

The cool early autumn wind whipped up and around our faces, alit from the lights above and around us. Soon I was alone with one of the young men. His tousled dirty blonde hair revealed cool ice blue eyes that looked at me with the kind of gaze that would melt the panties right off my ass if you know what I mean. Within moments we were kissing passionately. The kind of kiss I think that only Europeans know how to do. Dirty, raw, sensual. Both our mouths taste of beer and cigarettes. He unbuttoned my jeans and pulled them down to reveal thin red panties underneath. He slips them off too and lifts one of my legs up to rest on the columned railing as he descends down to kneel in front of me. I gazed out at the view of dazzling buildings in front of me. Contentedly puffing away at my smoke as this vision of Viking excellence orally pleasured me down below.

Y'all I didn't come here to write a smut novel but I had to share this because it was one of those moments that required a cinematic helicopter drive-by shot. My hair blowing in the wind, a hand on his head, overlooking the vast kingdom of the city that made me. A moment of limitlessness, a moment of sensuous pleasure. A moment of respite, a bite out of a timeline heading toward the depths of sorrow. We could all use moments like these along our paths of grief, do we not? Not to say the vices are totally necessary but, in certain cases I think they can be little helpers in breaking down the walls of our inhibitions, encouraging us to relax and receive. So, smoke if you got em' y'all!

WHAT THE WATER GAVE ME:

Clear. Cleanse. Purify.

NAME OF THE TOOL
What the Water Gave Me
Clear. Cleanse. Purify.

BRIEF DESCRIPTION

Connect with the healing properties of water

SET THE CONTAINER:

Go to a body of water, large or small. This could also be a bath. Submerge. Slow your breathing and embrace all aspects. Say this water prayer: Holy water that breathes me and moves within me. Let me be cleansed of all that worries my mind. All that I cannot understand and all that I do. Allow me to embrace the unknown and submerge myself within your dark waters. All that is known is at ease with my release. I honor you and you nourish me and all sentient beings. Thank you.

PRAYER /AFFIRMATION

I am at ONE with the healing properties of this water. I gratefully receive the abundant blessings and cleansing from this sacred spirit and element.

Imagine you're floating downstream. The sky hovers above you blue with a few fluffy clouds spattered here and there. The sun shines through and casts a light along the riverside that is both golden and fragmented. Like God is peeking out to shine through just for a moment of poetry for your eyes to feast on. You're on your back and all the cares in your world wash away. You feel full of release. No more need to control. Waves of cool water caress your body and all at once there's a feeling of being held and nothingness.

This is what I wish to impart on to you. There is nothing in the world like the feeling of water. And water comes to us in many ways. After all, we are made of 75% water, no? We are birthed out of a warm cocoon of fluid and most of what passes through us lives on for millennia just as the water that we drink today passed through the body of a stegosaurus on a hot summer afternoon thousands of years ago.

Water teaches us so much. The ability to freeze up and build fortitude, to become spacious and airy like the steam that rises off the pot of spaghetti you pour into the sink. We learn its fluidity through observation.

The lesson here is to embrace what water can teach us. What is that for you?

My wish for you is to embrace and dive in. Deeply fine-tuning yourself to the essence of water. The ways I suggest include taking yourself to a large body of water. Don't live near one? All good. Perhaps there is a stream or waterfall nearby. A fresh alpine lake perhaps? The idea is to find something you can fully submerge yourself into. I adore float tanks. They bring a magical sense of absolution. Like the Buddha who sat beneath the Bodhi tree, clearing themselves of all thoughts and merging with the absolute all here and now. Enlightening themselves with all beings.

This is your task.

When we face death and grief there is a sense of holding that comes. Of trying to grip on tightly to a sense of what 'reality is'. Though what happens when that fails? What can we hold on to with white knuckles when all that we know is slipping out of our fists?

The void.

The place of nothingness that exists within all things from the largest rock face cliffs of Yosemite, down to the atom that makes up the matter you currently call your wooden desk. Woah, does that scare you? I know. It scared me too when I first came across it at my own version of the Bodhi tree, the colorful woven Peruvian-rugged room of my Greenpoint, Brooklyn apartment. I watched all matter around me become a large nothingness as I saw the fabric of our reality is made up of a matter that we only collectively agree to exist within the vast confines of our own consciousness.

But how does this relate to water? You ask.

The water is an 'aqueous transmission' to quote Incubus. It is the closest I believe we can come to understanding the ultimate letting go and merging with the infinite.

> **"Clear water:**
> **No front**
> **No Back. "**
> –Chiyo-ni, Japanese Poet

Imagine you're floating on a river. Above you, a hawk flies, and beside you on the river bank your power animal strides along, watching as the current takes your body further downstream.

As the pace of the rushing water quickens, you come to understand that quite soon, you will be flung into the unknown, off the cliff of a waterfall into that which is unnameable or unknowable to you. Instead of clenching up. You allow and release. You soften all the bones and ligaments in your body. Your face softens and a small smile creeps across your face.

Yes, this too. All this is okay. Because the water told us so.

X MARKS THE SPOT:

Discovering Your Power Place

NAME OF THE TOOL
X Marks the Spot
Discovering Your Power Place

BRIEF DESCRIPTION

Visit your power place and establish your sacred place of ceremony.

SET THE CONTAINER

Just like buried treasure, find your power place. This is a spot where you can connect to your ancestors, spirit allies, and elemental guides. Create a sanctuary outdoors. This is your spot of reflection and connection. Like burying treasure, this is your sacred spot to honor your ancestors as well as mother earth.

PRAYER /AFFIRMATION

I AM connected. I AM HERE and I AM NOW. I am surrounded by a vortex of protection and Love. In this space I AM FREE.

X marks the spot, mateys! Like a pirate coming across a chest of riches after carefully following his treasure map, you've arrived here. But where? That is the question. When approaching our grieving practice it is crucial that we have power places where we feel at home. A designated place where we connect to the above, the within, the without, our nature allies and guiding spirits, our masters and ancestors.

A power spot is a place where we go to connect which can be a physical place or one that exists in the spirit world. Sometimes when a loved one departs we may choose to spend time at their grave site to connect with them, this is a wonderful option for a power place if it feels good for you. Otherwise, you may choose to add a selection of special spots that you go to seek refuge and do your spiritual work.

Some of my favorite power spot places include (but are not limited to):

Boulders

The thicker the better! Love a good ol' glacial boulder to chill with. If you think about it, these big beauties have been around for literal eons and have quite literally 'seen' it all. Try laying across one and tune into its energy. What messages does it have for you? How does it respond to your presence? Can you befriend this stone? Some rocks have been used for thousands of years by humans and you can tell by their vibration. Others have been chilling for a long time alone and might be a bit shy though could use the company. I find them to be great huggers, and teachers of steady patience & strength.

Rivers

Fresh, fresh, fresh! So lovely to have a river friend as a power place. A place of constant renewal and movement. The stones alongside make powerful friends for your altar. What do you release as you sit aside it? What songs come from your heart to the watery flow here? Try bathing in the waters to release.

Oceans

Big big momma, here we go! These behemoths are big-time teachers. They both hold and nurture life yet have the almighty power to extinguish it at their will. They carry vessels and sea life. What do the waves teach you? How do you feel when standing in front of its expanse?

Mountain tops

Powerful expansion! Arms open and held out wide to embrace the view! Have you ever tried yodeling on a mountain top? Great place to get perspective and see things from a bird's eye. Grounded nature. Wind medicine.

Fields

Shhh shhh shhh whispers the grasses as you run your fingers along their tips. Hmmm yes, what is here for you? Limitless possibility. A sense of what could be? How do the fields speak to you? What secrets do they hold?

Big ol' Trees

Wise breath keepers can be a friend for a day or a lifetime. Wonderful to respectfully introduce yourself to. Spend some time. Notice the ants crawling up the trunks. Notice the leaves swaying in the breeze. Notice the places where it's mending itself from a wound. Initials of past lovers carved into its skin. Forever regenerating slowly growing and observing. A friend for you.

When not visiting your power place physically you may choose to connect with one in the spirit world. Think of it as a spiritual meeting point where you can go to learn lessons, hang out with your animal allies, or meet with ancestors and guides. Listen to a shamanic journeying track while meditating with your eyes covered. Ask one of your allies to escort you to your medicinal power place in the ethers. You may be surprised by what you find! Spend some time there exploring its inner workings. What is its medicine? This is a great jumping-off place for other journeys. Get to know it well. You may choose to leave behind certain gifts or tools to be used later on. Bless it, caress it, anoint it with love and sage.

YOGA:

In Your Body, In Love

NAME OF THE TOOL
Yoga
In Your Body, In Love

BRIEF DESCRIPTION

Practicing physical asana is a way to remember Union. To Yoke the greatness that thou art.

SET THE CONTAINER

Whether it's a tried and true flow sequence or a daily sadhana, the physical aspect of yoga can be a great way to connect your mind and body together, which ultimately helps you to metabolize grief and other emotions in the body. Find a recording if you have trouble flowing into a natural sequence, or just let yourself go. If you've taken only a few classes, you'd be surprised how much your body knows how it needs to move. Yoga came spontaneously to the ancients before it became about choreography and moves. Same with dance. Same with magic. It's a deeper magic. And it's within you. Great news!

PRAYER /AFFIRMATION

I AM my knowing embodied. Through movement I rejoin the symphony.

Yoga means a lot of things to a lot of different people. Some believe it is joining upper middle-class white women in tight figure-hugging overpriced athleisure in a heated room, being instructed by a sculpted 20-something demi-god into shapes you never knew your body was (or should be) capable of. Sure, I have been that person. In a way. Others believe yoga is the practice of coming into a space, quieting the mind, finding a space of limitlessness, cleansing the body with asana, and poses to quiet the agitations we accumulate through our daily lives. Others believe yoga is this unattainable thing. This elusive one-ness that can be reached perhaps fleetingly for a moment. Touched upon, surely, but never fully grasped.

"I could never do yoga, I'm so inflexible!" I hear you saying. Yes, when I introduce myself as a yoga teacher this is often the reaction I get. But what I want you to know here is that the practice of yoga is many things and nothing at the same time. I often reply that the most advanced yogis I know do not practice any actual asana at all. To sit in quiet contemplation for over an hour to me is the most powerful and challenging practice. Think a headstand is advanced? Try superseding your egoic mind and coming into equanimity, brah.

I came to yoga after a fierce battle with my own body and mind. After years of extreme diets, and a twice-a-day gym rat habit, I was toasted. I needed a pathway to gain a friend within my body once more. I knew she was there, whispering lightly to me. A whisper on the wind when I stood atop a hill with my arms outstretched, ready to receive. There was another way, surely. I recall longingly gazing through yoga studio windows, at the women within, practicing quietly, and the sense of wisdom some of these practitioners seemed to hold. Yes, there was a slight wish to have that rockin' yoga bod (that niggling mind chatter that told me I had to look a certain way to be worthy). Surely. But there was another voice that told me this was a pathway to that freedom. To come into contact with that wise woman who stood on top of hills and spoke to the sky.

I was 19 when I went to my first class. I dragged my boyfriend's older, wiser, cooler sister to come with me. I was terrified. What if I didn't know the pose? And what do I wear? And will I be good at it? We entered the earthen-toned studio together. Me, clutching Dad's mossy green mat in hand. My boyfriend's sister went to Barnard and had been to Thailand, this wasn't even a blip on her social calendar of cool. She walked with an easeful grace that I felt so envious of. How to be this self-assured in a place I felt so out-of. The room smelled slightly of feet. I imagined the years of barefoot yogis practicing on the brown wall-to-wall carpeting had infused the place with an ever-blooming odor.

It wasn't offensive, it was somehow: human. Like the smell of my grandmother's cream-colored orthopedic summer sandals. Feet were my friends. A familiar smell that said, "you're welcome here, your feet probably smell too sometimes, and that is okay." Wow, what a relief! Gone was the fear of not being good enough. Gone was the paranoia I'd inhabited during my days of wanting to look like one of those Victoria's Secret magazine models. I felt a sense I was safe here. I was home.

That began a lifelong love affair with the practice. From the first "Om" I was totally enthralled. This was a place I could come, learn how to breathe into my body, be touched and nurtured by soothe-saying wisdom keeper practitioners, and at the end, what a treat! The teacher would rub gorgeous smelling essential oils over my shoulders and temples, completing this anointing with a gentle BOOP right onto my third eye at the center of my forehead. Was this enlightenment? I felt I was getting close. I found a practice to forgive my body. Finally, what sweet relief.

So I became a teacher of this craft. This way to harmonize, unionize, and pacify the self. I began teaching at my hometown studio, on Long Island's North Shore where elegant upper-middle-class moms rolled up in their escalades, ray-ban shades, and luxury athleisure wear. The Long Island yog-elite. At first glance, one might assume that these women had the same intentions I'd had initially: to get that hot rockin' MILF bod, and they were not wrong in that pursuit, no way. I get it.

But upon further diving into the teaching world, I discovered they were there for the same reasons I had found. To find that peace. I think we often have a misconception that with wealth comes ease, though I found it to be quite the opposite. These women still had their sorrows. Their divorces, their struggling children, the deaths of course of those they love. Life looked pristine and pottery-barned and Martha Stewart-esque perfection from the outside but their inner landscape was just as nuanced as the average 20-something struggling artist in Brooklyn.

Becoming a teacher led me to sharing this with people of all walks of life. I recall fondly teaching a group of neighborhood boys I'd met while staying in Detroit. Their bodies contorted to mirror my shapes in their baggy jeans and white t-shirts as cars drove by blasting Kendrick Lamar. I taught children with special needs who immediately tapped into the reservoir of stillness that comes with physical practice. There is something universal here. Once we demystify it and tell people, hey it's okay, you don't need to have to get your feet behind your head. Let's just move our bodies, people get it.

What am I trying to say? I believe yoga is for everyone. All walks of life, all abilities.

All around the world I find a home in these studios. A place to convene, connect, disconnect from time and mind, and be in touch with self. No matter the language spoken, we have a common tongue of practice. I can look into the eyes of a fellow yogi and know, they too have come seeking the salvation of self-inquiry.

For the beginner:

My advice to you is: do not freak out. I know the whole "Yoga" thing can seem super weird and inaccessible and pompous and all the things but I am here to tell you that no matter what size, shape, color, ability your body comes in: yoga is for you.

Start small. Find a local studio and check it out. See if you like the vibe. Pick up a schedule and maybe chat with a teacher. Ask what class would be best to start with.

Not quite ready to hit the studio? I gotchu. Plenty of online classes to pick from. I love YogaGlo for its affordable monthly subscription online platform. You can customize your search by level, effort, style, and duration.

Keep it short. You don't have to do a full 90-minute class right off the bat. Heck, even a 5-minute stretch/breath work/centering session does wonders for the soul.

Props. Are. Your Friend. Many of us make this mistake when first starting out (I know I did) in thinking that the less props you use, the more "advanced" you are. You may be thinking "but I'm young, limber, and strong. Heck, I did a 5k last month!" and while you're not wrong, and strong you may be, props are there to help support and guide the structure of your body. Think of it as scaffolding. You can still activate in a pose, if not more with a little bit of help from your friends (blocks, bolsters, blankets, straps). Plus huuuuge word to the wise: you are not impressing anyone by raw dogging your bare kneecaps on the hardwood floor in anjaneyasana. If it hurts, back off, grab a prop, and trust me: you'll feel a *lot* better.

Learn the difference between PAIN and sensation. Piggy-backing off the last point here, folks. There is a fine, fine line between these two bad boyz. We sometimes confuse deep sensation with pain because it can often be intertwined with enormous emotions (hello hip openers!) but this is where the juiciness of the present moment lies. Within your ability to be present with sensation and breathing into it.

When our friend pain comes to town: this wisdom also applies. This usually feels sharp, sometimes sudden, searing, nervy, you know the drill. It ain't fun! And while our egos may get involved and start saying: "Come on, ya wimp! Everyone else is doing it! We gotta be the BEST. Better than any other yogi in the room!" I hear you. But the truth is, your body is literally screaming for you to back off, grab a prop, or hell just skip the whole dang pose and chill in child's pose, down dog, or good ol' savasana til the next pose is introduced. I have spent entire CLASSES in a child's pose straight up chillin', and there is nothing wrong with that.

"Beginner's Mind" is literally envied by all seasoned yogis. For those who have been practicing for years, we all covet the mindset of the newly minted yogis, fresh-faced, and doe-eyed, with their beginner's yoga mats and soft foam blocks. The point is you're in the most wonderful time of your practice. You don't know all the names of poses or the "proper" alignment. You have no preconceived notions of what a "good" yoga class is, or how certain sequences should be arranged. Your body is still learning all these new forms, and your muscles have yet to build a memory yet of what they think certain poses should feel like. You may even just be tuning into entire organ systems and muscles, you never knew existed! (or had never previously paid much attention to) This is COOL guys. You are the cat's freakin' MEOW. We all want to learn from you. The insights you have as you develop your practice are golden and in fact, you should share them with the more seasoned yogis who think they know it all. Because the reality is, they don't! In fact, the most dedicated, studious, well-learned yogis I know who have practiced for over half their lives dedicate more time to unlearning. Coming back to the beginner's mind. Inquiry. Using our friends, PROPS, as their guides as they navigate their changing bodies and life circumstances.

To everything, there is a season. This goes for both beginners and the old yogi farts: there is a time and a place for all practices. Your practice this morning might not look like what your practice this evening is, or tomorrow, or next month, or five years from now. And that is A-okay, ya'll. Our bodies are meant to shift and change as we grow and age. Our job is to listen to it and adjust how we move and communicate with it. We can't expect to be the same all the time, and neither should our practice. So stay flexi, guys. And remember, it isn't that serious. Have fun with it!

To the seasoned practitioner, ask yourself a few questions:

- Where has my practice stagnated?
- Where have I been resisting growth?
- What teachers have I been resonating with?
- How do I need to shift my practice to accommodate my grief?
- In what areas does my practice need more discipline?
- In what areas does my practice need more space & softening?
- Can my practice of Yoga look different than it does now? How?
- What is a style I have been avoiding?

If I primarily practice a yang style (Ashtanga, vinyasa, hot yoga, etc) can I shift toward yin or restorative? Often I find we avoid the medicine we most need. When feelings become stagnant and we are ruminating within the emotion, I find my practice usually becomes languid, with long holds, and yin-like poses. While this is wonderful, and needed, I have to notice when things become too swayed in either direction. If I am avoiding feeling all the feels, and I try to keep the body and mind busy by fast-paced vinyasa practices, how can I notice this and choose to mindfully slow down and come back to presence? Shake it up, babies. Change your perspective. Sometimes a new way of seeing things is an inversion away.

Once again, my friends: Props. Are. Your friend. This one goes out to all y'all crunchy granolies out there who have been doing full lotus since you were a fetus and think you're god's gift to asana (who's to say you aren't though, really?). We can all learn a little something from calling out to our friends, the props. You thought this was just for the beginners? Oh no! I'm coming for you too! The lesson here is to get support where we need it. For too long we may have been torturing our bodies by overdoing things and could use a little grace. Supported pigeon anybody? Our perennial search for the peak pose can take a hike. Let's just be and get the feels we need right now. We don't have to be constantly reaching toward IG Yoga Model status like we're prepping for the yoga Olympics or something. Chiiiiilll babies. Make a pillow fort of bolsters/blankets/blocks and let yourself marinate in the bliss of our good friends. The Props.

Brief low down on different major styles of Yoga (in no particular order):

YIN

Poses are held longer (3-5 minutes) focusing on connective tissue/fascia instead of muscles. Think sphinx pose or seated forward fold held for a looong time. Wonderful for unwinding pent-up stuck-ness in the body. The ego/mind has to take a back seat and just chill.

WW**RESTORATIVE**

Similar in some ways to Yin, but different in its generous use of props to facilitate a relaxing, nourishing practice. Think eye pillows, reclined butterfly pose propped up on bolsters, covered in a blanket and sandbags. Wind chimes and singing bowls soundtrack.

YOGA NIDRA

Yoga nap, anyone? This goes out to my peeps who love to lounge. Or at least need to anyway. Having a tough time settling down after a long day of work? Or getting the body ready to sleep? Yoga Nidra is like a guided meditation to take you into deeper states of relaxation. Perfect for quieting the mind, releasing the day, and allowing the body to *rest*.

ASHTANGA/VINYASA

A faster-paced practice where one pose flows into the other usually by use of a vinyasa (plank, updog into down-dog). Usually comes with a lot of fun-looking acrobatics. Great to challenge the body and build up a sweat. Not so great for prolonged practice for the potential for injury if not practiced mindfully (in my opinion). Ashtanga is more regimented and follows a specific sequence and series. Great for masochists. Proceed at your own risk y'all, the ego loves this for its competitive nature and many of us have been down this rabbit hole only to end up with injuries. Great to learn a more disciplined style of practice & dedication. Find a good teacher who will support you in getting stronger and not push you into injury.

HATHA

Took me a while to understand that hatha is basically the broken-down poses on their own. Usually slower and more mindful. Loving it for taking time to tune in to the subtleties of the body. Simple. Usually taught by teachers who have pursued a more rigorous practice then learned how to break things down and approach it with more kindness.

KUNDALINI

Y'all I had to go there. Lots to say on this one and it is super polarizing though I would be remiss to mention this epic technique for working out your s-h-i-t. While it is marred with scandals (which at this point what yogic system isn't) but let's get real: these practices are freaking bomb. It doesn't follow the regular vinyasa or hatha style at all. The first time I was in class I wondered if I had stumbled into a cult (still not convinced I didn't). You practice on sheepskins and do various movements, breathing techniques, or "kriyas" along with chanting mantras. This supposedly burns off major karma. You find yourself pushing up against the barriers of your own egoic mind. It is brutal at times. Cathartic at others. And the high from all that pranayama is seriously unparalleled. Now the majorly f-ed up aspects of it that had me being pressured to constantly wear head-to-toe white, a full-on turban, and start going by my "Spiritual Name" left me with a major case of the heebie-jeebies. Don't let this scare you off entirely though! There are a handful of teachers with integrity who have pushed aside the weird culty dogma and are embracing a more measured and practical approach to the style. If anyone tells you that in order to practice you need to look, sound, or be called by a certain name: run. Otherwise, it is absolutely epic and you'll find yourself reaching new levels of spiritual attainment, connection, and bliss consciousness. You win some, you lose some?

LAUGHTER YOGA

A wonderful method of laughing your way into happiness. Look up a few how-to videos online or find a local class. Looks absolutely ridiculous. Feels strangely amazing. The techniques they use employ what I view as clowning around but sure enough, after a few minutes, you'll find yourself actually laughing and feeling more joyful. They say laughter is the best medicine, you know!

CRYING YOGA

On the flip side is what I call Crying Yoga which is a rather untapped resource though widely known in some ways. We often find the hugest release of emotion in our yoga practice. Ever spontaneously broken down in tears after a heart opener? Sometimes we resist pulling the plug on big scary emotions because that is just what they are, big and scary! It can be helpful to be in a safe container to really let them loose. Ever notice how a toddler will sometimes cry and whine even when nothing is actually really "wrong"?

This style is releasing pent-up emotions that don't necessarily have to connect with any particular experience. We just carry this stuff around with us and we need to, as adults, let ourselves be whiny babies sometimes. During your at-home practice, play around with whimpering, even "fake" crying when you go into a deep pose where you feel emotional resistance. Often the imitation of crying gives the body a cue that it is safe to let loose and really do a big ugly cry. Try it out and let me know what you think!

To all yogis:

Boop! I gave you a little third eye lavender oil anointing. Just because. Love you. Forever with you on the cosmic highway yoga mat, practicing next to you in spirit.

A couple of things the yogis have taught me that helped me deal with grief:

On the Breath

Big topic here y'all but I'm gonna try to say a few things about it. Life begins and ends with the breath. It sounds super simple and in a lot of ways, it is. Though what I am more interested in is layers between that simplicity. The liminal space that lies between each inhale and each exhale we take. As yogis (or living beings really) we may take our breath for granted. A lot of the time it is unconscious. We don't really notice it. And that is where my practice came into view. I had been hearing over and over by different teachers about the importance of breath. "Listen to your breath. Don't do anything to try and change it, just notice it. Inhale. Exhale. Inhale for a count of four. Retain the breath. Exhale for a count of four. Retain the exhale."

All my teachers had been yammering on about the breath and I felt that I "got it". But I realized I had only scratched the surface of the enormous gargantuan importance that breath plays in our life. By examining the place it has in our death did I get to more fully grasp the intricacies in the poetry that each breath has in store for us. Maybe you understand it in this way, too.

At the bedside of my father's hospice bed, I would sit each night. Counting his breaths. I would listen carefully to each inhale then hold my breath for the pause. The pause of an eternity. The pause was a luxurious limbo that was both here and not at all. The pause meant that from this moment to the next, life could be changed in that instant. How wonderful! How strange. How nebulous.

And I started to time each inhale and exhale. Because sure enough after what seemed an interminable amount of time after each exhale there would come this earth-shattering inhale that screamed: "YES, I am still here. Breath is within me again." And then, moments later the exhale would come. And the waiting began again. Over and over and over throughout each night, I would sit. Sometimes watching with a stopwatch. Counting the ticks of time, from tick to tock, between the inhale, the exhale, and the revivifying inhale again. Like small deaths over and over.

This made me see how fragile and magnificent life is. That we are all but one moment, one breath away from limitlessness. Eternity is between each inhale, and each exhale. Poetic, yes. Something to investigate? Maybe. Something to cherish? I think so.

More than anything this lesson brought me into a deeper connection with my own breathing practice. Pranayama offers us a gateway to come into great connection with that life-giving gaseous elixir that oxygen brings to us.

My advice here? Pay attention to your breath. Nurture it. And not only yours but thank the breath keepers of our earth. The trees! The plants and the bees that keep it all going. We are a circle of life and what we give, others take, and what others take, we give. Inhale and exhale.

Colonics AKA Colon Cleanse

Okay, kids, I wouldn't be the true Virgo Queen I am without talking to you about butt stuff. One of my all-time fave things to do is get the old booty hole cleaned. "Why?" I hear you beg, pleading with me to please just skip this entire part of the chapter. But no! I'm here to regale the delicious experience that a colon cleanse has to offer. Something the wise ancient yogis of yore came up with that has been passed down generation to generation, butt hole to butt hole. Yes, my friends. Back in the day our yogi friends clad in their small loincloth diaper outfits (I assume this was the attire) would head down to the river and clean their bottoms.

That's right, the French were not the only freaks on the streets with their bidets, oh no. Our yogi friends would squat down and practice Jala Basti. Using the technique of Uddiyana Bandha, they'd suck river water up into their anus and hold it, maybe move it around a bit by undulating their bellies, and when the time was ripe, out with the old and in with the new! Off went their excrement and any other impurities. We hold old toxic waste in our bodies and colons and it can be super helpful to clean out the ol' booty hole and the good news is, these days you don't have to go down to the local river to do it! That's right, you can visit your friendly colon cleanser or colon hydrotherapist to help you out. Often there are great deals for coupons and I recommend buying a few in a pack so you're prepped.

"Why!?" Again I hear you plead with your fingers intertwined, on your knees even. I know. We're getting there, patience.

The idea here is that not only are there nasty toxins all balled up in there with last month's steak dinner but more importantly there are huuuuuge emotions stuck up in there too! We carry deep feelings all over our bodies which we can work to transmute with movement practice, proper nutrition, good water, breath, etc. But often even with the best of intentions, we can become, for lack of a better term "full of sh*t".

Stuck in our emotions, perhaps holding on to memories and experiences. I know. Ever had that grief constipation? I think it is a by-product of the fight or flight situation we get ourselves into over grief. That feeling of either needing to immediately evacuate all avenues when feeling the proximity of death or the holding on for dear life and not letting go, white-knuckling it kind of complete digestion stop up. No good.

Some people go to therapy every week (which is great don't get me wrong). For me, I am for colon hydrotherapy all the way. My colon hydrotherapist became my BFF as I came in nearly every week for a certain period of time after Dad's death. Her name is Estella and she is a kind-hearted Puerto Rican grandmother. The kind of person you'd want to hold your hand while releasing deep grief. She'd look me in the eyes and say "Elenita, you're really full of it this week". And she'd rub my belly and my feet as I would cry and scream and sometimes even sing opera at the top of my lungs while expelling smol pellets of built-up resentments/anger/etc from my bottom. Don Giovanni anyone?

Okay there, I've said it all. Find your local colonic spot, hit them up. It takes a small amount of discomfort and a minuscule learning curve to get over pooping in front of a stranger but your body and your digestive system will thank you for it later. Also if you're a freak like me, you'll find a strange pleasure in seeing all the weird things that come out. Did I go too far? Oh well.

Sauna

Get. In. One. Had to include this in the chapter on yoga because it is something I learned through my practice.

In the autumn after falling in love with yoga, I headed to London to study abroad. At the time the practice was a fairly new phenomenon in western culture and studios were sparse. I trialed which spots I could find though I hadn't quite locked into any one spot. Craving the practice deeply I thought: "some practice is better than none", which is how I ended up doing a *certain* style you all may be familiar with. Heated room. Mirrored walls. Teachers yelling instructions through microphones and maneuvering you into the deepest expression of each pose (regardless of whether your body was ready for it or not).

And let's just throw in some sexual harassment lawsuits regarding its flashy founder. I think you all know who I'm talking about by now, right? We won't speak its name here, but you get the gist. So in short I was sweating my nonexistent balls off every day literally commuting an hour each way from North London, down to central London, then up to Camden to get my yoga fix in. Why am I telling you all this? Sounds horrible, doesn't it? It was and it wasn't. I learned to fall in love with sweating. Coming from a woman who never did team sports and the most I ever sweated was a dainty light glisten even during the height of my gym rat days. I was sweat averse. I had always felt uncomfortable, and icky as soon as I began sweating. But this practice of being in the heat shifted things. Suddenly I embraced the release of this strange clear liquid from my body. It felt like a baptism of sweat.

Each week I would stare down at my legs and watch small rivers of sweat run off to the towel beneath my feet. The clarity of my mind was unparalleled. My skin felt soft and supple. I glowed. After each class, all the women showered together in this large open-aired shower which I found fantastic! I'd never been around women who were so unashamed of their bodies. Was it a European thing? I'd never seen American women act so freely in a public restroom. All around me were bodies of all shapes and sizes. All kinds of boobs and pubic hairstyles. Shaved, unshaved. Landing strip here, full Brazilian there. I was in heaven (and not for freaky reasons, if that is what you're thinking). I felt that this sweating thing was so innate and needed within our culture. To sweat together felt like a holy communion so-to-speak. And since then I have sought it out in any iteration it is served in.

Call me a bathhouse fiend, why don't you. I am now fully obsessed with Korean spas. The benefits of saunas are many and while I could go on about this, I won't bore you with the sciency details (that is what google is for). Think of it: your body is given a chance to release all the pent-up B.S it has been storing. Overdid it on the wine the other night? Sweat it out. Had a few too many french fries and feel greasy? Sweat it out! Just feeling super funky and not sure how to shift it? Sweat it out! That's something you won't read on a medical explanation of why saunas are amazing. Not only does sweating allow the body to clean itself out, again it gives us the opportunity to process our (say it with me kids) EMOTIONS. Yup. That's right y'all.

Half the time when I was resisting sweating I realized I was just resisting the release of big-time feels that I'd been carrying. The moment the body is given permission to release, it ALL comes up to be healed and washed away. And the best part is, you don't have to talk to anyone while you're in there. You can go in, get into your zone, go into a deep meditation. Massage your body, rub it all down. Slap the sh*t out of it to awaken all the cells (this feels seriously really, really good) and get those toxins moving and on their way! Buh-bye! I feel like I could write an entire tome on the joys of Korean spas but I'll save that for the next book.

ZOUNDS!

God's Wounds: This Too Shall Pass

NAME OF THE TOOL
Zounds!
God's Wounds: This Too Shall Pass

BRIEF DESCRIPTION

Imagine that for a moment, this moment is not all there is. That you can have a future that feels less awful than this moment. This wounding. This loss. A willingness to imagine a future of joy and fullness. Of new.

SET THE CONTAINER

Make your space around you one that invites you to let go. For some, this could mean being in bed with covers up and a fave blanket. For others, this could mean dropping in on your yoga mat with a candle and incense lit. The most important thing is to feel safe enough to let go.

PRAYER /AFFIRMATION

This is not all there is. I am not this wound. I am not this loss. I am love incarnate, and my future self, wise and wonderful, can meet me here to usher me into greater understanding.

Time Heals All Wounds

Zounds literally translates to "God's Wounds" and is often delightfully used during Shakespearean drama. Sort of like how we often say today when exasperated: "Jesus Christ!" Reminds me often of this little lesson I learned. An acting teacher once instructed me and my high school theater class that whenever you've forgotten a line while you're on stage, that you could always just exclaim with gusto: "Time heals all wounds"!

I've got to say it is a tried and true tactic for dealing with just about anything in life.

Whenever you're doubting the process and feeling like you may just be going out of your mind, remember: time heals all wounds! I remember after my first true heartbreak, my high school boyfriend, I would go on these long drives through my hometown where our love story had unfolded, blasting really intense musical theater love songs and just drowning in a sense of hopelessness. I knew that I looked ridiculous to anyone I passed by on my route. Tears ran down my face, trying to belt songs out to match the high notes of Lea Salonga (impossible) but of course, it was what I needed to get through it. And I have to say, it helped.

What I wish I could have told my teenage self was that this too shall pass. I remember waking up one day and having that realization, of course, it was after it was all over. Sometimes we have to go through the muck to get that wisdom, you know? Sometimes the cut is so deep, we can't imagine that life can exist on the other side of loss, pain, heartbreak, betrayal, etc. But it does. Sometimes it takes longer than we have the understanding for, but there is renewal, grace, and something (and someone) even better.

It was helpful to know that at some point all the hurt would not be as intense. It is hard to fathom during a breakup, or when you are in grief. When going through a loss of love or loved one, there are countless mornings that you will wake up, and perhaps for those first few waking moments, you will have forgotten. You have simply woken up, your eyes open to focus on the room around you. You notice the sunlight peeking through the window, you feel the cushiness of the duvet that is around you, you feel yourself new into the day and then ... it happens: you remember.

Suddenly that feeling of overwhelming dread for all things takes over you. You realize once more, that yes, they are gone. And no, they won't be coming back. I know: you feel like there is absolutely no reason now to get out of bed, let alone brush your teeth, or put on clothes. What is the point? The world may seem dark and like there is no other possible way to view things. I know. Your loved one is gone and the world is sh*t and your bed is maybe the only nice thing about your current circumstances. Maybe sleep a little more? 14 hours of sleep never hurt anyone, right? Right.

Ladies and gents, I am here as a survivor to tell you that yes, you too shall arise one day and you will feel one thing: alive. There will come a day where you will wake up, and your first thought will only be that of: "time for coffee". This is to say that yes, time will come where you can begin your day and feel that you have once again regained a sense of 'self' outside of the grief. Outside of the experience that once defined you.

I also want to remind you of something if you're still in the thick of it. Perhaps you're still in anticipatory grief. All you need to do is breathe and allow.

Time for a Little Meditation

Find yourself in this current space. Notice where you're at. See yourself in this current time and place. Breathe.

Remember that time is an illusion. You are simultaneously here in this current moment, and at the same time, you are but a baby being held in the arms of your loved one. You are going to your first day of kindergarten. You're tasting your first tropical fruit. You're having your first kiss. You're graduating from high school and college. Look at you go! You have already done and experienced so much in this life it is truly remarkable. I want to invite you now to the future. In this future, it is absolutely certain: that you will see this day. In the future there you are in your morning. New into the day. You're there making your morning cup of coffee and you feel so incredibly YOU that there is no other thing to do but to smile and relish in it. You have the feeling that anything is possible today. Today you will go places, meet new people, and have a sense of possibility that is unparalleled.

You are content. You feel unburdened and alive. This day is here and now ... yes it lives in the future but it is THERE for you and waiting for your most delightful arrival. I promise you this with complete certainty because I am living this moment now as I write to you perched on a balcony in the hills of Topanga outside of Los Angeles, a few years after my father's passing. Today I woke up, in the arms of my lover, and after a few morning breath kisses, the first thought I had was: "I can't wait for my first cup of coffee".

Time heals all wounds. This too shall pass. I don't say this to you to say that you will never again cry over the loss of your loved one. Of course. The wind may blow and you'll feel again like a pile of leaves just blowing away. A song will come on the radio that will have you sobbing all over like it has just happened. Yes. The grief will always be with you. The memory of them will always be with you. But soon, I promise you: their memory will become like a friend that rides with you always. Soon, the essence of your loved one will guide you and make you laugh more than it will make you cry. You'll delight in knowing that they are always with you. The wisdom that they imparted onto you. Their jokes, their taste in music or fashion, will light your path and be like a funny companion.

These days I find I am laughing more with the thought of my Dad than crying over him. I'm telling you this though I know no matter what I say, it will not take away from the pain of this moment. I know no combination of words will ease your suffering. But I am just here as a beacon to light the way. To show you, it gets easier.

I made it here — and you will too. It is certain.

Time heals all wounds. And one day, you'll wake up both better for the deepening of the experience. More because of it. To be holy is to become hallowed. For you have been visited by the master initiator itself: Holy Death.

In the paradox of opening fully to loss, grief, and this howling curriculum of life, is a larger capacity for life itself. You won't be who you were on the other side of it. But by making the choice to say yes to your crazy wisdom within, to bring forth your inner death doula and glamorous God-self, you may just come out the other side with the kind of wild wisdom that touches, inspires, and flips your entire existence on its sparkly, delightful head.

EPILOGUE:

Guru as Garbage Dump

Every day I visit a wooded area of my hometown with my dog. As I have been writing this book it has been a safe haven for me. A place to go every day where I can be alone and be with the trees. They have no judgment of me. I can arrive in whatever state I am in. Disheveled. Glamorous. Whatever. Nature sees me as me and it is there that I can shed any layers holding me back. Any layers of shame, guilt, apprehension, and most importantly: grief. In moments of supreme pain, I can lean on my tree's branches. I ask their help in holding it all when it feels like too much. The funny thing is, this land has been a garbage dump for the last however many decades.

Only recently was it converted to mountain biking trails. I especially love to run up and down with my little doggie. It is lush with tangled vines, twisting and unruly. Amidst the branches, the large glacial boulders, and sandy knolls are strange artifacts of times before. A beer can there, half a car there, a gigantic truck tire piled against an old stove. Long tunnel-like cement cylinders line the walkway. Strewn between stones are remnants of an old mop. Strange and fluffy. It witnesses me.

I see that nature is trying. It is rebirthing itself. As it swallows the rejected bits of humanity and transmutes it. Turning an old washing machine into a planting bed. A home for small rabbits. Within these wild paths, I see that it has a history it tells as I walk. Long before it was a place to store forgotten things it was a place of great industry. The cracks and large dips within the sandy earth tells a story of what came before.

The sand from this land was mined to build all the streets of New York City. Recalling the line I learned that spurred on the mass emigration through Ellis Island that America's streets were "paved with gold". Those promising streets beckoned my own family who arrived on steam liners to escape Civil War in Spain. The streets of New York have a history of their own. And a poetry that many artists, musicians, politicians, and more have built their legacies off of. Those streets somehow though always deeply rooted in my hometown. I remind myself of this as I walk alone on the city streets. No matter where I go in that city I am always home. The sand beneath my feet is the sand that birthed me. The place I call home. And long before the mining and dissection of that land, it was held by the Matinecock people. Their memories have since been erased from time and paved over with colonial reminiscence of "George Washington slept here."

How curious to think of a place secured in time. How one plot of land can hold so many stories. How like old cathedrals passing through caretakers over centuries one layer is built on top of another. Pyramid on top of pyramid. Sacred land once. Desecrated the next. Sanctified again by a young woman and her dog passing by the rusted spindles of a bike wheel, wedged into the side of a growing tree like molten lava.

I sing as I walk the land of my Guru Garbage Dump. As I go it teaches me. As I go, I sing and tell the land that it is doing just fine. I see the long vines wrapping around and crushing the things that people from the past thought were meaningless. Making meaning out of mud. Making meaning out of struggle. Creating poetry through time. I see that even though a space served so many people then abandoned and trashed, it could always rebuild itself into something new. I see life teeming around me. The birds don't care much to see old steel beams swallowed by the earth. They sing their songs anyway and I sing back. Together we sing the song of hope for healing. As we sing and twirl our notes around one another so too do the vines, wrapping up and up and the roots digging down way below. I sense the land knows its time is coming again. Like the next wave of patience has proven its might. The glacial boulders laugh. Their staying power is that of reigning dynasties while the trees in their short-sighted wisdom say excitedly: "Look! Look at how we're healing!"

I wonder if the Guru is teaching me about myself. I see myself as a garbage dump. Once sacred land, then torn apart at the seams to build a great city. A city that holds the heartbreak, the history, the heritage of a nation. My body is that nation. Through the pain of loss, I've built something great. And while parts of me are spread wide around the world through my travels, I come back to my fertile ground. I see the old parts of me strewn about like constant reminders of who I once was and where I came from. Sifting through the discarded relics of the past in my childhood home, I see that certain things that hurt to see have now become a part of me. I swirl a fresh green vine around my father's moss-colored fleece jacket.

A leaf shades our childhood photos. My grandparent's furniture supports my back as I find serenity and sit like the queen I have become. My own forest of recycled things. My own guru-like garbage dump. Somehow now though completely whole. No longer trying to clean up or sanitize the self. No longer harboring feelings of unworthiness that told me I would never be good enough, clean enough, successful enough. I could just be: enough. With the places, spaces, and things that made me, me. Sure, it's a bit jagged in spots though I would take that over a manicured falsity any day.

Next to the garbage dump guru appropriately sits a golf course. Occasionally I let my dog run wild across its perfectly undulating fields. I secretly hope she poops. A hawk watches overhead as she chases a great blue heron into flight. Here too is God. I glance back at my Guru, she smiles, beckoning me back into her lush womb.

I return to lay my body face down across a Glacial Boulder. A wise wisdom keeper that tells me, yes child, come home and lay yourself down. Pause, get still. Know that you are perfect in the here and now. Nothing needs to be changed. Patience as you allow. Liken yourself to lichen. Fertile soil will follow. You, my child, are wise, as you hold the magnitude of the life you've led. No need to brush it aside. Let it become you.

And with that, I bid adieu to this eon of my life writing this book. I trust it will change and the way I feel about my words will too as I age. Though my hope will remain that it becomes a part of me, like a smashed-up teacup. I repair the cracks with gold and pour it all out.

My hope for you, dear reader, is that you take this opportunity to see yourself, too, as a Guru Garbage Dump. Forever recreating the self. Forever replenishing, reinventing, rewilding. Forever changing and growing as you meet life's challenges head-on. Death does not define you, dear one. You will triumph over this because there is no end. As the snake eats its own tail, so do we.

So put on your sunglasses and your most fabulous fit, and get out there. Share yourself with the world and dare to dream larger. Dare to be that thing you've been hiding away. Dare to show your most fabulous, messy, and wild self. The world needs you, dear Grief Walker. The depths you've navigated are like a badge of honor or a banged-up old dryer to add to your trophy wall in your own garbage dump. Weave the vines around it and let it heal into a new being.

I want to leave you all with something really poetic and lovely though the truth is, the lawn chair I'm sitting in is making my bottom unbelievably itchy and so with that, dear ones, I bid you adieu. See you in the spirit world. You'll find me with a cup of tea, a long skinny cigarette, red lipstick, and black shades. Ta-ta for now.

Made in the USA
Middletown, DE
15 February 2022

61025142R10142